OXFORD WORLD'S CLASSICS

ALIS AL-BUSTANI

Sa'ïba

Translated with an Introduction and Notes by
MARILYN BOOTH

OXFORD
UNIVERSITY PRESS

Great Clarendon Street, Oxford, OX2 6DP,
United Kingdom

Oxford University Press is a department of the University of Oxford. It furthers the University's objective of excellence in research, scholarship, and education by publishing worldwide. Oxford is a registered trade mark of Oxford University Press in the UK and in certain other countries.

Published in the United States of America by Oxford University Press
198 Madison Avenue, New York, NY 10016, United States of America

British Library Cataloguing in Publication Data
Data available

Library of Congress Control Number: 2025932765

ISBN 9780198921684

Printed and bound in the UK by
Clays Ltd, Elcograf S.p.A.

The manufacturer's authorised representative in the EU for product safety is Oxford University Press España S.A. of Parque Empresarial San Fernando de Henares, Avenida de Castilla, 2 – 28830 Madrid (www.oup.es/en or product.safety@oup.com). OUP España S.A. also acts as importer into Spain of products made by the manufacturer.

The manufacturer's authorised representative in the EU for product safety is Oxford University Press España S.A. of El Parque Empresarial San Fernando de Henares, Avenida de Castilla, 2 – 28830 Madrid (www.oup.es/en or product.safety@oup.com). OUP España S.A. also acts as importer into Spain of products made by the manufacturer.

OXFORD WORLD'S CLASSICS

SA'IBA

ALIS BUTRUS AL-BUSTANI was born in Beirut in 1870 into an illustrious family of writers and educators, the eleventh and final child of the renowned educator and writer Butrus al-Bustani and his equally energetic and well-educated spouse Rahil 'Ata al-Bustani. Educated in Beirut, in a school associated with American Protestant missionaries, Alis would have been well-versed in Arabic letters as well as having a familiarity with English-language literature. In 1891, her only known work of fiction, *Sa'iba*, was published in Beirut. She married her cousin 'Abdallah al-Bustani, a physician, and after several years in Lebanon they immigrated to Cairo with their young son Nabil. Alis died in Cairo in 1926 and is buried in the Maronite cemetery there.

MARILYN BOOTH is Professor Emerita at the University of Oxford and Fellow of Magdalen College, Oxford. She was holder through 2023 of an endowed chair in contemporary Arab studies, and previously held a chair in Arabic and Islamic Studies at the University of Edinburgh. Her published work focuses on nineteenth-century Arabophone women's writing and ideologies of gender debate, including the role of translation. Recent research fellowships include the Institute for Advanced Study, Princeton; l'Institut d'études avancées, Paris; Neubauer Collegium for Society and Culture, Chicago. She was visiting professor, l'EHESS, Paris, in 2024. She has translated many works of Arabic fiction into English.

OXFORD WORLD'S CLASSICS

For over 100 years Oxford World's Classics have brought readers closer to the world's great literature. Now with over 700 titles—from the 4,000-year-old myths of Mesopotamia to the twentieth century's greatest novels—the series makes available lesser-known as well as celebrated writing.

The pocket-sized hardbacks of the early years contained introductions by Virginia Woolf, T. S. Eliot, Graham Greene, and other literary figures which enriched the experience of reading. Today the series is recognized for its fine scholarship and reliability in texts that span world literature, drama and poetry, religion, philosophy, and politics. Each edition includes perceptive commentary and essential background information to meet the changing needs of readers.

CONTENTS

ACKNOWLEDGEMENTS

I AM thankful for the support and encouragement of Samir Bustany, Alis al-Bustani's grandson, as I pursued this project. I am also grateful to Samir and his brothers for the biographical information and images they supplied. Samir and other members of the Bustany family have given strong support to initiatives aimed at archiving and highlighting the achievements of their remarkable clan. Equally, I want to thank Kamran Rastegar for urging this project in the first place, and bringing me into contact with Samir. Finally, I thank colleagues who have generously provided information and advice on references and intertexts, from Molière to Salonica: Ellen Fleischmann, Fabio Giomi, Suzanne Jones, Christine Lindner, Yaseen Noorani, Kamran Rastegar, Holly Shissler, Johann Strauss, and Stefano Taglia. I am particularly grateful to Johann Strauss for his thorough and good-natured help with Ottoman references and spellings.

Marilyn Booth
Oxford
November 2024

INTRODUCTION

ALIS AL-BUSTANI (1870–1926) was 21 years old when her first and only novel was published in Beirut. She prefaced it with a flowery dedication to the Ottoman Sultan, in two languages—Arabic and Ottoman Turkish. This encomium thanked him for his attention to schooling the Empire's girls and boys, in an era when new girls' schools had begun to produce a wider female readership, across Arabic-speaking, Turkish-speaking, and other Ottoman-language communities. *Sa'iba* is one of the first published long fictions known to be authored by an Arabophone woman. It is Alis al-Bustani's only known published composition save for a brief oration in honour of her mother, delivered before schoolgirls and teachers in 1894 and published soon thereafter.

It was appropriate to provide a bilingual dedication, not only out of respect for the sultan but because this is an Arabic novel about Turkish-speaking characters. A genre that would become recognizable as the Arabic novel had emerged in the mid-nineteenth century in Arabophone provinces of the Ottoman Empire, specifically the cities of Ottoman Syria, and notably Beirut with its energetic private-publishing scene. Fiction added its voices to the intellectual and political ferment of the time. By 1891, the gendered organization of society was a key theme in public debate among the small but growing lettered population. Women were participating in public debate (in print), forming women's discussion groups, and advocating for more educational opportunity. Questions of gender and generation—especially the rights of the young to make their own life choices—were the backbone of the early Arabic novel as they were elsewhere. Girls' education and shifting marriage practices, overlain by the question of patriarchal authority in the family and polity, drive this novel's plot and character formation.

The era encompassing the early nineteenth century to the onset of the First World War became known as the Nahda ('awakening', 'getting-to-one's-feet', often translated as 'renaissance'). This was a movement concerned with knowledge- and institution-building among educated Arabs in conversation with similar movements within and beyond the Ottoman Empire. The Nahda's cultural momentum drew in ever-expanding audiences for newspapers (listeners as well as readers), theatre, and other arts. The Nahda challenged persistent Orientalist stereotypes of passivity and cultural 'belatedness' as characteristic of the region's people. Nahda activists cogitated on myriad cultural, political, social, and economic aspirations and stresses. In this reformist context, gender rights and relations were central issues. 'Women's rights' (*huquq al-nisa'*), a contentious and variously defined concept, were a key dilemma at the centre of a desired modernity, entangled with aspirations for political independence and local economic vitality in the era of high European colonialism.

Egypt (to which Alis would move later in life) and historic Syria (comprising the present-day countries at the eastern end of the Mediterranean) were the early centres of cultural activity. But the Nahda emerged amongst conflicting political forces. Nine years before Alis al-Bustani's novel came out in Beirut, British troops had occupied Egypt, following growing state debt seen as threatening the interests of European creditors, and political unrest arising from native Egyptians' sense of exclusion from the Turkish-dominant ruling structure. Along both sides of the Mediterranean, and throughout the nineteenth century, Ottomans witnessed European encroachments and local breakaway movements. Algeria, Morocco, and Tunisia were under French colonial rule. Alis's home territory, the Ottoman Levant, had seen incursions by Egyptian, French, and British forces. The Greeks had achieved independence, and Balkan populations were in ferment, encouraged by the Russian state.

The Ottoman world was a multilingual cosmopolitan space. Arabic learning was paramount to her family, but Alis also encountered English. Her father—famous educationist, writer-translator, and editor Butrus al-Bustani (1819–83)—had translated *Robinson Crusoe* and worked with American missionaries; her mother had grown up partly in an Anglophone missionary household where—as a young girl—she served as an interpreter. Our author was probably somewhat familiar with the literature of both Britain and North America. Nourished on the venerable literary tradition of her native tongue, no doubt she also partook of the recent flourishing of Arabic novels. Her two oldest siblings were early contributors to Arabic fiction. Alis al-Bustani's novel, composed in Arabic and set mostly in Istanbul, displays Arabic, Ottoman, and British Victorian resonances. It demonstrates a strong consciousness of the centrality of gendered social institutions to the shape of society and its reform, in the Ottoman Empire as in Victorian Britain or Third-Republic France.

Sa'iba reaches beyond questions of law, custom, and familiar everyday practice to probe the persistence of attitudes that worked against change: ideas about women, men, and 'nature' that even reform-minded people found hard to discard. Alis al-Bustani drew on a wide range of cultural, geographic, and political resonances. *Sa'iba* is an early feminist work in that it portrays not only a young woman's struggle to have her say, but also the moral and psychological pain, and the possibility of tragedy, that accrue when women's word is discounted.[1] What, it asks, constitutes 'honour' in a quickly changing world? If women were supposed to learn new ways of being—to bear a representational burden of 'modernity' by managing new models of wifehood and motherhood—then how must men, and concepts of 'good masculinity', change as well? After all, women also bore the burden of patriarchal expectations and sedimented ideas about 'feminine nature', including their exclusion from public-political subjecthood.

An Arabic Novel

Women participated in the emergence of modern fiction in Arabic. From 1888 to the onset of the First World War, women published at least thirteen novels, numerous short stories (many translated or adapted from European languages), and eight translated novels. (More may have done so, anonymously or under masculine names.)

These were exciting times for would-be writers. Expanded transportation and communication networks—railway lines, steamships, and the telegraph—intensified global contact. Printing opportunities were growing. In the eighteenth century, entrepreneurial intellectuals had founded printing businesses. The nineteenth century witnessed the emergence of a broader print scene, while a manuscript-based culture continued to circulate texts old and new. In Egypt in the early 1820s, a state printing press at Bulaq (in Cairo) began fulfilling the aspirations of Egypt's bold Ottoman governor, Mehmet Ali (or

[1] Fruma Zachs takes a similar perspective in 'Subversive Voices of Daughters of the *Nahda*: Alice al-Bustani and *Riwayat Sa'iba* (1891)', *Hawwa: Journal of Women of the Middle East and the Islamic World* 9 (2011), 332–57.

Muhammad 'Ali, ruled 1805–48). Producing scientific and pedagogic manuals for medical-school and military-college students, gradually it expanded to printing poetry collections, creative prose, and biography. It published some of the earliest texts authored by women of the modern era.

From mid-century, a private printing and publishing industry centred in Cairo, Alexandria, Aleppo, and Beirut issued contemporary and earlier works while staying afloat by printing visiting cards, popular tales, colloquial poetry, and songs. Printer-publishers—such as Alis's brother-in-law Khalil Sarkis (1842–1915), who would publish her novel—founded newspapers and magazines, creating a symbiosis between serial publication and the business of printing. Print culture spread to provincial towns and villages, and to immigrant communities in Europe and the Americas. Emigration had intensified due to political strife and economic hardship in Ottoman Syria, and a regime stepping up political repression and censorship. Some editor-publishers moved to the less constrained venue of Egypt. There, emigrant Syrians and native Egyptians gained additional income by printing novels on their presses and advertising or featuring them in their periodicals. Magazine editors were also novelists and translators. Arabic periodicals were hybrid in content. Early political newspapers, such as *al-Ahram* (est. 1876), like Beirut's earlier *Hadiqat al-akhbar* (est. 1858), published fiction, including a novel by another al-Bustani, Sa'id (d. 1901), *Dhat al-khidr* (She the Secluded, 1884). Like many other debut novels, it focused on the issue of arranged marriage.

Print culture was sustained by emerging cultural institutions that built on older patterns while responding to new conditions. Across the Ottoman Empire, education expanded due to local-individual and government-sponsored initiatives. Missionaries from Britain, France, and the United States also founded schools, welcomed cautiously by the state. If literacy levels were low, the number of readers was growing—and more people were able to purchase books and magazines. This included female readers, for girls' schools were appearing, though at a lower rate than schools for boys. (Both girls and boys had long attended *kuttab*s, basic Qur'an schools where recitation, some grammar, and writing were learnt; or the equivalents in Christian communities.) When he translated *Robinson Crusoe*, Alis's father felt a need to acknowledge female readership as a new force. In his preface, Butrus al-Bustani remarked that *Robinson Crusoe*—and his rendition of it—'because it is refined and polite, will find a welcoming audience in this era in which the doors to education have opened to women, too; and in which we must attend to cleaning up the ancient Arabs' poetic and prose works, ridding them of inappropriate words and actions, out of respect for the modesty and proper safeguarding of this sex'.[2]

Pedagogic needs fuelled publishing ventures. By *Sa'iba*'s publication, books destined for school use had been appearing in Arabic for nearly two decades. Echoing this novel's rhetoric on education, schoolbooks included declarations of education's importance. They highlighted the significance of girls' schooling for a modern society with chapters on household management (*tadbir al-manzil*) and child-raising (*tarbiya*)—terms that *Sa'iba* deploys. Novelists claimed pedagogic territory, too, justifying fiction as a means to offer appealing moral guidance that young readers might avoid if presented in other, drier, forms. In his preface to *She the Secluded*, Sa'id al-Bustani declared, 'It has become clear from experience that the art of novels is amongst the best means of moral training (*tarbiya*): novels provide exemplary models and wisdom crafted to offer the mind repose and the heart delight.'[3] But what was the best mode of *tarbiya*? Should parents (and authors) allow their teenagers to read only 'exemplary' texts in the sense that Sa'id al-Bustani appeared to suggest? Should they banish narratives that touched on various temptations that (commentators worried) loomed large in the Empire's cities—from sex work to gambling and alcohol consumption to new nightlife venues—and on human deception and 'moral corruption'? Or, ought writers expose the young to these realities—to negative exemplarity—as a means of steering them along healthier pathways? Novelistic 'enjoyment' must be didactically useful, novelists urged. They did so rather defensively, it must be said: the darker sides of human

[2] Butrus al-Bustani, 'Muqaddimat al-mutarjim', *Kitab al-tuhfa al-Bustaniyya fi al-asfar al-karuziyya, aw Rihlat Rubinsun Karuzi*, part one (3rd printing, Beirut: al-Matba'a al-amrikiyya, 1904), unpaginated. All translations from Arabic are by M. Booth.

[3] Sa'id al-Bustani, preface to *Dhat al-khidr*, in Muhammad Sayyid 'Abd al-Tawwab, *Nazariyyat al-riwaya al-'arabiyya: al-Muqaddimat al-ula min sanat 1858–1914* (Cairo: al-Hay'a al-'amma lil-kitab, 2010), 48, giving an 1880 publication date (on p. 176, 1884 is given). *Dhat al-khidr* is a now-obsolete epithet for a female at or beyond puberty and connotes socioeconomic status that would make seclusion possible.

behaviour were more likely to grip readers than were edifying tales of 'good girls'.

The novel afforded creative space to individuals who didn't have the 'high' literary or religious training of earlier (and almost entirely male) intellectual elites (though writers outside religious-scholarly circles existed in earlier times, too). On title pages (male) novelists defined themselves as schoolteachers, students, engineers, or government bureaucrats. Yet, as publishers issued one novel after another, contributors to periodicals expressed anxiety about the popularity of *romans:* the borrowed French term connoted romance novels. These commentators feared the impact *romans* might have on young readers, especially girls.

As the usage *roman* suggests, the perils of novels were perceived as imported—in both a social and a narrative sense. Some commentators referred darkly to 'French novels' as a dangerous contagion (echoing concurrent debates in Britain). The boundary between 'original', 'adapted', and 'translated' fiction was blurry. The novel was also nourished by earlier Arabic creative forms such as the popular *sira* (heroic epic), though critics at the time tried to distinguish these tales from the 'sober' didactic novel. It's no accident that in *Sa'iba*, young Farid grew up on 'tales of chivalry', while the heroine's education focused on grammar, rhetoric, and homemaking. Careful *tarbiya* has produced a sensible, grounded young woman. Lack of it has produced a young man who is at best personally dissipated and at worst destructive of the rewoven social fabric that reformists sought to produce.

Novels were recognized as particularly apt teaching tools when formal education remained restricted. Writers were sensitive to readers' limitations and lack of worldly experience. Women writing novels focused on what they believed women and girls needed to learn. Compatriots who had not enjoyed the benefits of sustained education 'deserve writers' concern, for they need amusing, easy-to-follow material that they enjoy reading. . . . Novels might be the best channel . . . especially in these lands where ignorance prevails. The market for foolishness is vast while the trade in high literature fails', in the words of essayist, novelist, and translator Labiba Hashim (1882–1947), writing in 1903.[4] Novels couldn't do this work alone. Hashim and

[4] Labiba Hashim, 'Taqriz wa-intiqad', *Anis al-jalis* 6: 5 (30 April 1903), 417–20.

other women urged parents to put their daughters in school, to let them stay in school longer, and to contribute to founding new schools—as Alis al-Bustani's parents had done in Beirut, seven years before her birth.

A few women had gained renown as published poets and essayists. 'A'isha Taymur (1840–1903) in Egypt and Warda al-Yaziji (1838–1924) in Lebanon hailed from intellectual households and were educated by fathers, brothers, and extensive family libraries. They gave explicit recognition to the strong tradition in ancient Arabic letters of women's poetic excellence. These families—Taymurs, Yazijis, Bustanis, and others—viewed writing and contributing to new cultural institutions as key contributions to the society's vitality. Their book prefaces often expressed a sense of social, cultural, and religious duty.

Political tensions, social change, and new infrastructures made cultural work—intellectual production and publishing, setting up schools and associations, challenging everyday habitudes—appear possible and necessary. The Nahda—invoking a rich past, dynamic present, and hopeful future—was a collective (though often individually pursued) and consciously performed expression of this view, a bid to 'revive' Arabic letters and 'awaken' Arab societies. Writers exhorted their peers to join a new cultural mission: creating a modern, outwardly looking and inwardly sourced, society. Making educational opportunities for the young—girls and boys—and producing reading material for them and their elders were high on the list of must-dos. Families like the Bustanis were engaged in all aspects of this mission. *Sa'iba* attests to the primacy—and excitement—of the venture, the sense of possibility that those who might have felt excluded from writing (and reading) could entertain. In her 'Dedication', Alis al-Bustani recognized this as she spoke for a rising group of readers: 'the community of women...granted the light of knowledge, in this era so well-fortified by learning'.

Editors acknowledged this emerging female constituency, as readers and as writers. Beirut's prominent newspaper *Lisan al-hal*, quoting from another newspaper, *al-Ittihad*, trumpeted *Sa'iba* as evidence of women's literary activism 'in these recent years'; women's presence in the literary sphere was a barometer of society's progress, these and other newspapers declared. Epithets describing women writers were conventional, but in this reformist milieu, they took on new resonance: *fadilat*, excellent or virtuous women; *muhsinat*, 'protected' or 'fortressed' and hence respectable (translated below as 'esteemed'). By showing respect for these writers, the paper(s) performatively reminded readers that female writers *were* respectable.

These days, it cannot be doubted that anyone perusing compositions by Eastern women—their writings on literature, morals, and sciences—will be persuaded that before the next quarter century passes across our Eastern lands, [these women] will have moved from their present condition to the highest possible level of achievement. In these recent years, our newspapers have been filled with productions from the pens of the most excellent amongst our esteemed women. Today, we received a novel, *Sa'iba*, composed by the fine literary writer al-Sayyida Alis, daughter of the late Butrus al-Bustani. It is a moral-literary narrative on pure love, preserving affections and guarding honour, and the consequences faced by the corrupt, who fail to succeed. We wish we could describe further this novel's fine qualities, but space does not permit. In sum, it is a worthwhile read and merits readers' approbation. It testifies to the writer's refinement and abundant excellence.[5]

Alis's novel, and early fiction by her female contemporaries, were proof-texts for those who defended women's intellectual endeavours against doubters. Sadly, this was necessary. About five weeks before *Lisan* recommended her novel, a reader wrote in on the theme of female achievement as a marker of social progress. 'Ottoman Women in the Hamidian Era' saluted both Turkish-speaking and Arabic-speaking female intellectuals. Mentioning *Sa'iba*, it parallels the novel's emphasis on education. Typically, it links female schooling (as the novel does) to women's family-oriented work as their contribution to their homeland. The anonymous author defined himself (using masculine-gendered terms) as a Beiruti yet also as 'amongst foreigners born in the protective shade of the Ottoman Sultan's realm'.

Among basic, self-evident truths, obvious to anyone who has studied history, is that the advance of a nation's women is the significant proof and clear sign that this nation has attained the heights of success—of being-civilized—and comprehends what true success means. How could it be otherwise, since woman is pillar of the family and cornerstone of society? Her character forms children's moral foundation; her learned culture refines and educates them. Of her a famous man of wisdom said—and he

[5] 'Ju'bat *al-Lisan: al-Ittihad*' (*Al-Lisan*'s Quiver: From *al-Ittihad* [newspaper]', *Lisan al-hal* 15: 1394 (23 March 1892), 2.

got it right—that the one who rocks the cradle with one hand rocks the world with the other.[6] In the Ottoman nation's uplift in its golden Hamidian era, we have the greatest proof of how true these words are. Everyone who reads Ottoman newspapers, Arabic and Turkish, sees—as I do—that the pens of Ottoman women occupy an important place and are recognized. Likewise, they have observed—as I have—that as women's compositional style has grown stronger and the content of their articles more refined, the nation has striven ever more actively towards success, mounting the upward route of civilization. This confirms that Ottoman women's advance echoes the progress of their community; rather, it is the [community's] companion on this path—indeed, it is the primary factor.

This advance [is so obvious] that any attempt to deny it is like trying to deny the sun's existence... here are the women of Istanbul, writing on scientific and literary subjects, and on economics, just like the West's finest female writers. They compose valuable books and translate works of benefit to their lands. Notice how the women of Syria have stepped as boldly into the writing arena as Turkish women have—wielding pens like burnished swords, with insights that hit home [*sa'ibat*]. Here is one who gifts readers of her country a series of articles on 'Work', which she has translated... another delights the ear with articles on 'Child-raising', while over here is someone with a valuable speech titled 'Our Uplift'. And then, another woman, with a novel—a first—entitled *Sa'iba*, aiming to commend good moral behaviour and reject what is reprehensible.[7]

Praising these writers, 'the Beiruti' went on to give a vivid example of many men's inability to believe that women could write such polished prose. Alis's novel, though, was noticed by other leading periodicals. *Al-Muqtataf* (founded in Beirut in 1876, published in Cairo from 1885) recognized the work's novelty and linked it to the prodigious intellectual profile of Alis's father, a rather patriarchal tribute to the work that reminds us of the structures and strictures within which women wrote.

The House of Bustani simply will not occupy any position other than that of precedent, in every contemporary literary field. The well-remembered

[6] This saying has been associated with Butrus al-Bustani in his 1849 lecture on female education or perhaps only in its 1870s republication in his journal; the likely source was an English-language poem first published in 1865. (Christine B. Lindner, 'Rahil 'Ata al-Bustani, Wife and Mother of the Nahda', in Adel Beshara (ed.), *Butrus al-Bustani: Spirit of the Age* (Melbourne: IPhoenixPublishing, 2014), 49–67; 66, 382 n. 146, citing work by S. Halevi and F. Zachs). See Appendix 1 for another evocation of this aphorism.

[7] 'Al-Sayyidat al-'uthmaniyyat fi al-'asr al-Hamidi', *Lisan al-hal* 15: 1383 (15 February 1892), 3.

and late lamented Butrus Efendi al-Bustani preceded sons of his era in producing [his works].... No wonder we see one of his daughters preceding her peers in writing a fictional narrative, Arabic in form and Eastern in subject.

Paging through this novel, we found it the ultimate in delicacy, sensitivity, and harmony. It explicates how women fare in the elite Ottoman family. It urges refined behaviour and virtuous comportment, and warns against consequences of immoral and foolish acts, and the corrupt characters of certain riffraff who warp Easterners' morals in order to profit from their money. The novel takes place in Sublime Istanbul. It ends grievously... the woman at its centre is seen as a model of chaste behaviour and respectfulness, intelligence and refinement; but her cousin's stupidity wrecks the peaceful joy of her life as it arouses rancour in her husband's heart. And then [the cousin's folly] snatches her away... just when her husband has become certain of her innocence and purity.

This novel is offered to His Sublime Majesty as one fruit of His compassion for women, exercised in the founding of schools to educate and refine them.[8]

This precis blamed the story's denouement on 'riffraff'—implicitly the character Boulos, a savvy Ottoman Greek. The novel does open itself to this reading, and participates in common stereotypes of the time, but it doesn't put the blame on Boulos. He is an accomplice. The chief culprits are the poorly educated, coddled son of an Ottoman Turkish family and the attitudes that produced him—the formation of his character.

Titles, 'Character', and the Connubial

Al-Bustani's novel shares a common feature of novels focused on women's experiences—if not necessarily on women's perspectives—in early Arabic fiction: titling practices. A high proportion of novels in Arabic (translated, adapted, or original) published before 1914 bore the names of female protagonists or—more often—epithets of female sexual-social status and physical appearance. The spotlight was on young and unmarried (more accurately, to-be-married) female protagonists. Such titles also alerted readers that romance would move the story: *The Gazelle of Tanta*, *The Berlin Lovely*, *The Virgin of*

[8] 'Bab al-hadaya wa-al-taqariz', *al-Muqtataf* 16: 7 (April 1892), 495–7; 'Riwayat Sa'iba', 496.

Quraysh, *The Beautiful Circassian*, *Young Woman of the Bosphorus*, *European Girl in the East*, *The Virgin of Japan*, *The Tunisian Enchantress.*

Sa'iba takes the metaphorical possibilities of this practice in a different direction, but by using an eponymous title, it doesn't do away with epithetic description. The title/name Sa'iba ('Correct', 'Apposite'; 'Well-Aimed') is the quality marking out the heroine as exemplary. Was the author lampooning the ubiquity of physically descriptive titles? *Sa'iba* highlights morals and character rather than physical (or geographical) titillation, while proposing an individual woman's selfhood.

Some chose distinctly different titles: *Maka'id al-rijal*, for instance, 'the ruses of men', was the title of an 1886 novel adapted by Shakir Shuqayr. Verses on the title page of this work published by a venerable church-affiliated press reminded readers that everyone could learn from reading novels:

> Stories are a treasure of benefit true;
>   The clueless gain reason and the knowing, decorum
> Guard their truths well, let their sage words accrue:
>   Secrets opening doors to a worldly-wise forum.[9]

Ruses inflect *Sa'iba*, too. Al-Bustani plays with a persistent misogynous belief in *kayd al-nisa'*, 'women's wiliness' or trickery, an enduring association of femaleness with deception or underhandedness, a concept in premodern Arabic sources. Wiliness was a prized attribute of folk-epic heroes (including a few female characters), but usually when applied to women it took on a negative meaning and was often sexualized. In *Sa'iba*, *kayd* is instigated by *men* who use patriarchal assumptions to trick and harm women. The equation of females with 'wiles' was argued against in other women's fiction in this era. 'A'isha Taymur's *The Results of Circumstances in Words and Deeds* (1888), rewriting the premodern 'mirrors for princes' genre, highlighted the ruses of men trying to captivate young Prince Mamduh in their bid for power. There's another interesting convergence: Taymur has Mamduh's wise handlers select Buran as a potential spouse who can exert rational influence over a wayward young man—as Farid's mother hopes Sa'iba will do.

[9] Shakir Shuqayr, *Riwayat makayid al-rijal* (Beirut: Matba'at al-Qadis Jawarjiyus (St Georgios), 1886), unpaginated. We are not told what this is an adaptation (*ta'rib*, 'Arabization') of.

But even seductive titles, and *kayd*, were not deployed only to titillate or warn young readers. These novels often introduced issues of public concern, crystallized in marriage practices. How much choice in marital partner should the young have, and how much contact should they have with prospective spouses? At what age should girls leave school and prepare for their married futures? (Almost all discussion assumed this as a woman's inevitable, or at least ideal, future.) When would parents stop pushing their young daughters into marriages with much older—and wealthier—men? What were married women's rights? If laws were in place to protect those rights, were they implemented, in the face of males' socioeconomic and juridical primacy? The tensions between individuals' desires and patriarchal family marriage arrangements generated discussions in periodicals and formed the plots in the early Arabic-language theatre. One novel after another—wherever and whenever the story might be set—embraced these unresolved questions. From the 1870s or earlier, with novels by Alis's brother Salim (1846–84) and others, such fictions enacted critiques of arranged marriages and sketched stark scenarios of forced 'unions'.

*Roman*s centring on tragic love stories and sometimes based on European works were often set in earlier historical periods or distant (exotic) locales. The vehicle of translation allowed bold new ideas to be presented at a cultural distance. But these, too, of course, constituted a local and contemporary commentary on gender politics. Some educated state employees, a growing group across the Empire, as well as independent professional men, sought educated wives—as companions, homemakers, and child-raisers, and perhaps as social partners, though elite and middle-class society remained greatly homosocial. Were these men ready to accept educated women's expectations for their own lives? Were they ready to shed old prejudices against female 'nature'? In this context—as in Victorian Britain and elsewhere—'romance novels' were political, and not only because in some (including *Sa'iba*) romance was intertwined with politically tinged intrigue. They were about 'character', a topic that filled front-page newspaper columns.

In Alis's mother Rahil's training (see Appendix 1), and in the novel's description of the women of an Istanbul family, we see models of educated women. Book-learned, they are also consummate domestic managers for whom 'character' is all-important. It must be so, given the strong expectations on women to be carriers of family honour, a discipline Sa'iba learns and embodies at home and in school.

Novels subjected assumptions about femininity and masculinity to scrutiny. Images of masculinity within patriarchal social formations might pit older, received notions of masculine behaviour against newer habitudes. Often, what drove a plot were competing notions of 'modern' masculinity. In *Sa'iba*, Farid's assumptions about time-honoured entitlement, as Sa'iba's first cousin, are buttressed (incongruously?) by his self-image as a modern young man-about-town with a Europeanized veneer. His cousin Sa'iba chooses a very different kind of man as her marriage partner, against the wishes of her mother and her aunt. (Both are widowed, allowing readers to recognize the roles older women play in maintaining patriarchal understandings of privilege—while the notable absence of fathers implicitly allows all characters more latitude.) In many other early Arabic novels, female characters insist on their own marriage choices. Sometimes this entails recognizing the truly virtuous and egalitarian-minded man. Other times, it results in disastrous misrecognition. Such novels challenged culturally and religiously sanctioned presumptions of masculine authority based on men's allegedly greater understanding and virtue[10] that governed the Ottoman social landscape—as it did (and does) so many other societies. *Sa'iba* is particularly nuanced. It turns a spotlight on reformist platitudes of the time—and thus on the limits to 'enlightened masculinity' in a society governed by patriarchal structures and assumptions.

If males were open to criticism in these novels, ultimately it was on and through female bodies, and social expectations of 'femininity' that the story rested. Novelists highlighted the social, psychological, and physical suffering of women. If this made women's and girls' pain impossible to ignore, it could leave masculinity in the background, a silenced issue. In the press, women were often blamed for society's 'backwardness'. Sometimes, focusing on women's experiences and outlooks in fiction may have contributed to erasing men's roles in this 'backwardness'.

[10] Madeline C. Zilfi makes this point well in her *Women and Slavery in the Late Ottoman Empire: The Design of Difference* (Cambridge: Cambridge University Press, 2010), 19.

Novels' authors were aware of—and participated in—debates in print swirling around these issues. From paratextual material it is clear that they were written consciously as gender-aware fiction, an alternative archive of material histories of women's experiences between family, law, custom, and national reputation. Novels reflect, test, and reshape understandings of identity, community mores, and beliefs about gender at a given historical moment—including the ways patriarchal structures offer comfort as they impose violence. As a social institution, the novel was as formative in late colonial Arab societies as it was elsewhere, in India, North and South America, Japan, or Europe. Novels complicated the polemics of 'East' versus 'West', which were often represented in the press as opposing images of gendered behaviour: the 'freedom' of 'the West' versus the constraint of 'the East'. A novel, on the other hand, might show local communities and practices both as allowing women's agency and as obstacles to their self-realization, while also criticizing certain notions of 'freedom'. The formulaic nature of much fiction produced at the time allowed new conversations to inhabit familiar forms. These included stock figures and melodramatic plots of oral storytellers, and the not-so-different features of European adventure fiction, fast becoming familiar fare through its translation-adaptation into Arabic (and Turkish). As Labiba Hashim and others recognized, for young women whose formal education ended early, or who were taught at home, fiction might provide an interesting secondary curriculum, alongside biography and the conduct-texts that proliferated then.

A Novel of the 1890s

Although al-Bustani's novel shows the imprint of early Arabic fictional practice—stereotyped figures, melodramatic events, awkward temporal and spatial transitions—it also stands out from it. *Sa'iba* contains very little poetry (in contrast to novels by female peers 'A'isha Taymur and Zaynab Fawwaz). It shares the didactic cast of other early Arabic novels (especially in observations on marriage practices and female education), but is unusually reliant on lively dialogue. It eschews the traditional dialogue marker *qalat*/*qala* (she/he said), using dashes to indicate speech. Unusually, it opens with a conversation among women; and Fahima is narrator of her sister's and niece's story. With the second chapter's description of the Ottoman social-educational landscape, Fahima's voice blends into the voice of an omniscient narrator, but that first framing sets the story as one told from a female character's perspective. This opening valorizes women's oral knowledge networks—what some male authors of the time denigrated as 'women's gossip'.

Certain moments display narrative clunkiness (for twenty-first-century readers), reminding us that writers (and readers) were new to long fiction. In using occasional direct address to the reader, al-Bustani and others drew on oral storytellers' strategies of hailing listeners, gently familiarizing readers with a genre still new to Arabic. (Another borrowing from the storytellers' toolbox is the loaded description of characters: Farid is a consummate if naïve urban chameleon-trickster.)

The decision to begin with a female narrator internal to the story, even if punctuated by an author-figure's interventions, pushed against a persistent social norm: silence as women's sphere. But it also makes good sense. We learn the back-story, and the narrative up to Sa'iba's and Lutfi's wedding, from the women's conversation. We meet the other characters first through Fahima's eyes; only later do we see events through other viewpoints, with a shift from the older generation to the younger. The young people's necessarily limited knowledges and internal struggles allow both sympathy and critique.

Set in a time of social transition, the novel traces the intricacies of gendered behaviour and its spatial correlates: what the women wear to go outside the home; how wedding celebrations are separated into male-only and female-only spaces. If these patterns were followed in elite Muslim households more strenuously than in Christian ones, they remained pertinent to both (including Alis al-Bustani's Protestant family of Maronite origin). One didactic, direct-address moment in the novel comprises an explanation of 'Eastern' versus 'Western' betrothal practices. The passage's exposure of 'Eastern' women's vulnerabilities in a patriarchal marriage institution—where young women are expected to be 'malleable', and where men retain privilege through law and custom—would have been relevant to Ottomans of all communities.

Beginning in a women's domestic world, the novel moves outwards: these well-off urban women are not enclosed within the home. They are not the secluded females of either an Orientalist imagination or an older, and variable, elite domestic configuration. Changing gender mores are evident. The women go shopping and hire a boat for an excursion on the Bosphorus. If this would have been more possible for older (and especially widowed) women, the young protagonist, after her marriage, drives her own chaise. Yet, such 'freedom' of movement reveals the narrow confines of expectation and possibility within which urban Ottoman women of a privileged class acted, even at this *fin-de-siècle* moment.

The Dedication signals an agenda: the necessity and benefits of strong formal female education. The female characters are introduced through a description of the setting: the interior of an old and comfortable, elite but not ostentatious, home, indicative of 'good taste' and sensible feminine management, explained pointedly as the outcome of Istanbul's 'fine schooling for girls'. Readers would have recognized in the description the value of continuity but also the modern via these exemplary educated women who meld old and new, and the well-schooled girl who articulates her own choices (to the consternation of her elders!). As in many British novels of the era, the history is there as a backdrop; the focus is on the politics of what happens at home.

Issues of 'honour' as represented in women's self-segregation from male-occupied spaces are central to the plot. (As in other early novels by women, bad masculinity is revealed by an intemperate young man's willingness to invade feminine space.) *Sa'iba* is concerned with moral training. Undisciplined upbringing (explained in many newspaper articles as the fault of uneducated mothers) is paired with destructive masculinity. Sa'iba's excellent training, academically and in home management, contrasts with her cousin's rudimentary skills, nourished by fanciful romance stories. The picture of a young rake, he may remind readers of Anthony Trollope's Felix in *The Way We Live Now*, although, as far as we know, Farid, as a young Muslim, indulges in gambling and a dandyish appearance but not in alcohol. He is a global 'type' of the era—the young male wastrel. As in Trollope's novel, the indulgent mother who cannot face up to her son's sly indolence is also a target of criticism. Farid's mother believes marriage to a good woman (as opposed to a wealthy woman, for which Felix's mother yearns) is the best way forward, and she relies on the accepted custom of first-cousin marriage. But Sa'iba refuses to play the role of mother/educator to her badly raised cousin, while—unlike him—she is observant about family members' feelings. In her one published speech, Alis al-Bustani subscribed to the elite consensus on the importance of learned motherhood.[11] But here, she signals that women's own wishes for romantic and intellectual fulfilment are as important as their duties to family and society.

Meanwhile, we are introduced to Lutfi Bey, diligent graduate of the Ottoman Empire's foremost military academy. Lutfi Bey's home overlooks the garden of Sa'iba's home. He falls in love with the sight of her—although elite Muslims' gender-segregation ideals would have made even a garden sighting unusual. But he is even more impressed by her stellar reputation. As Lutfi and Farid represent opposing models of masculinity, the values associated with Lutfi suggest the ascendancy of a bourgeois ethos based on older local values and also linked socially and economically to the ruling Ottoman regime. Lutfi is a product and beneficiary of the spreading bureaucratic elite. He is a newspaper reader, but he is also rooted in longstanding structures of belonging. From 'an old family', he has a carefully maintained income from real estate as well as a military post, plus he has the intelligence to 'ward off the gamesters eager for his money'. A modern man attracted to an educated woman, Lutfi finds himself caught in stereotypes that brand women as susceptible and deceitful. *Sa'iba*'s plot turns on men's deceptions, particularly in luring a woman into a closed space, and thus exploiting notions of 'honour' by placing her in a compromising situation. Sa'iba challenges masculine 'honour' by reminding Farid that, as a relation, he ought to be the first to protect female family members. She thus tries to turn to advantage the notion of patriarchal 'honour' as resting on control—euphemistically, 'protection'—of female sexuality (and reputation). Farid responds that the power is in her hands, when they both know full well that he can ruin her. Even as she exposes the 'ruses' of patriarchal ideology, Sa'iba is uncomfortably aware that she must play along with Farid's patriarchal game if she is to have a hope of survival.

If the novel is organized through a series of melodramatic events, it delves into the human psyche to a degree unusual in early Arabic fictions. Characters struggle with the understandings on which they were raised. Lutfi believes his wife is 'sincere and pure', and yet he

[11] Analysed by Deanna Ferree Womack in *Protestants, Gender and the Arab Renaissance in Late Ottoman Syria* (Edinburgh: Edinburgh University Press, 2019), 174–6.

cannot ignore what he (thought he) saw. Sa'iba hopes desperately that Lutfi will trust and believe her, but she also knows that appearances, however unfair, are socially meaningful. Farid, immature and woebegone, is more pitiful than detestable—but he has the power to ruin the female cousin who has spurned him.

Alis's older siblings treated similar issues, and created somewhat similar characters, in their fictions. Alis's sister Idlid (Adelaide, 1839–1933) wrote a novella published in a family-run magazine the year Alis was born that confronted similar 'dilemmas in women's lives' to those Sa'iba faces.[12] Her brother Salim's novels addressed these issues. His fourth novel (*Asma'*, 1873) was the first with a contemporary and local setting. (Like *Sa'iba*, it bore an eponymous title.) He constructed characters whose outlines were echoed in his younger sister's fictional couple. Karim ('generous' or 'honourable'), the intellectually minded hero, is 'wealthy but not materialistic', and is not conventionally handsome—traits that Alis's Lutfi exhibits. Salim's Asma' is highly educated and a trained domestic manager. The counter-character—named Farid—manifests superficial interest in European culture—its attire but not its literature.[13] *Asma'* and *Sa'iba* focus on marriage partner choice as crucial to personal happiness and to a thriving modern society.

If it differs from most novels of its era and before in its lively dialogue, eschewal of poetry, and interiority, *Sa'iba* does resort to 'stock characters'—local stereotypes—of the time: the scheming, ne'er-do-well Greek fixer Boulos and the female accomplice, Marjana. Such figures appeared repeatedly in popular storytelling, from colloquial satirical narrative poetry to heroic epic (linking Farid's boyhood reading to his present scheming). Marjana—a figure from the Ali Baba story (in some later versions of *Thousand and One Nights*) but with echoes of the Fata Morgana figure of European legend—is also the *jariya*, the (former?) slave in the household. She is a 'part' of the household but forever dependent and degraded. She must cultivate her future by cultivating those with (patriarchal and financial) power, however flimsy it might be, as in Farid's case. Boulos, in a different

[12] Zachs, 'Subversive Voices', 344, 345–6. Zachs notes that Salim's characters, unlike Alis's, are 'two-dimensional' (p. 346).

[13] Sharon Halevi and Fruma Zachs, '*Asma* (1873): The Early Arabic Novel as Social Compass', *Studies in the Novel* 39: 4 (Winter 2007), 416–30; 424.

way, is vulnerable in a society where he has no formal status. His fanciful card-playing suggests the precarity of his condition. In al-Bustani's novel, these stereotypical characters also draw sympathy. Nonetheless, unlike other characters, Marjana and Boulos display little to no interiority.

An Ottoman Novel?

Sa'iba takes place not among Arabic-speaking communities in Beirut or Cairo, but largely in the Ottoman capital. Like other authors, Alis al-Bustani may have felt that she could best present a critical lens on contemporary and local women's lives by displacing her story. From a Christian family, she took the unusual step of creating implicitly Muslim protagonists (though their faith identity is not to the fore, and the main characters bear names that are not specific to one religion or the other). Perhaps she felt more comfortable portraying Muslim characters 'at a distance'. There may have been other reasons. As suggested by the *Lisan al-hal* letter quoted earlier, in the Arabic press there was recognition that middle-class and elite urban women in Istanbul had got further than had most of their peers in the cities of Syria and Egypt in exercising expanding prerogatives: education, mobility through public space, the production of women's journals. (The earliest Arabic women's journal would appear the year after *Sa'iba*'s publication.) Some elite Turkish Muslim families had begun to favour more publicly visible sociability for women, earlier than did most Arab Muslim families. Imagining modern, mobile, educated women, al-Bustani could most convincingly show these women in an Istanbul setting. Perhaps, also, she could 'test the waters' as to Arabic readers' attitudes toward elite and middle-class shifts in gendered expectations without ruffling too many readerly feathers.

Novels in other Ottoman languages emerged decades before Alis's novel appeared. Questions of marriage, morality, and public behaviour loomed large in these works. There is no indication that *Sa'iba* was ever translated into Ottoman Turkish, but it would have offered themes familiar to Ottoman Turkish readers, and a highly credible social landscape.

As noted, the Arabic movement for cultural regeneration, yielding new cultural institutions, emerged in the context of reform processes across the Empire, though initiatives of intellectuals in Beirut,

Aleppo, Cairo, and elsewhere were firmly local. Sa'iba's father (and then her husband) are employed in the rapidly expanding civil service and military structure—the centralized bureaucracy associated with what was known as the Tanzimat ('Orderings'), the nineteenth-century push for reform and modernization led by the Ottoman state. This began officially with an 1839 state decree and led to a complex series of administrative and legislative reforms as well as attitudinal shifts.[14] From the late eighteenth century, Ottoman sultans and their advisors had confronted various levels of European penetration: political pressures (partly by encouraging ethnically based minority separatist movements), military inroads, and economic challenges. The regime had responded with changes to security structures. The Tanzimat formalized an ongoing process that entailed both fragmentation of a multi-ethnic elite and new notions of belonging. While it did not do away with the authority of community (religious) leaders over their constituencies, it did posit a notion of individual subjecthood: Ottoman subjects as citizens, with rights and duties. This was in tension with the regime's increasing centralization, and particularly the autocratic outlook of the modernizing nineteenth-century sultans. Ironically, in destroying older centres of power and building a new bureaucracy—together with modern schools—the sultans facilitated new opposition, including a short-lived constitution (1876), suspended by the incoming sultan in the context of conflict with imperial Russia.

Abdülhamid II reigned when Alis was writing (1876–1909). His rule generated opposition over time: his bid to tighten control while practising selective institutional change became increasingly autocratic and focused on security. However, he was recognized—and lauded—as having expanded his predecessors' focus on establishing educational institutions, including girls' schools. His own daughters were educated—though their school was on the palace grounds.[15]

In 'Mrs Max Müller's' 1897 travelogue, her husband, an Orientalist scholar who contributed several chapters, mentioned education as he

[14] What the Tanzimat was envisioned to do, and what these reforms meant for the Empire, has been the subject of much scholarship. See Select Bibliography: Late Ottoman history.

[15] An affecting portrait of his concern with their learning occurs in the memoirs of his daughter Ayşe (1887–1960), composed in the 1950s. The passage is translated in Douglas Scott Brookes (trans. and ed.), *The Concubine, the Princess, and the Teacher: Voices from the Ottoman Harem* (Austin: University of Texas Press, 2008), 149–51.

described the Müllers' visit to Istanbul in the early 1890s. The details may be exuberant more than they are accurate, but they suggest that this top-down attention to learning was lauded outside the Empire.

It is pleasant to see crowds of children, both girls and boys, going to school, as in England. The schools are public and elementary. Most of them owe their origin to the initiative of the reigning Sultan, who is sowing seed of which others will reap the harvest. Strong and determined was the opposition of the conservative and more particularly of the clerical party to the establishment of public elementary schools. The Sultan had to found them himself, and has to support them out of his own private income.[16]

The 1839 Gülhane Decree initiating the Tanzimat proclaimed the equal status of different population groups in an empire where Muslims had been the paramount subjects. Ottoman (including Arabophone) reformers, members of minority groups (such as the Bustani family), and, increasingly, a movement opposing the sultan's authoritarian rule, might take this as encouragement to assert individual rights—and women's rights. As in the Arabophone provinces, the press, and fiction, were key loci for debate. Attempting to balance his 'westernizing' reforms with a strong focus on his authority as based in Islamic precepts of the just ruler, Abdülhamid II used the press, both fostering and censoring debate.[17]

Late-Ottoman schooling produced a modernizing elite, concerned with women's rights, and produced journalism by and for women. The first generation of published female writers and editors were women from families of the ruling elite, such as Fatma Aliye (1862–1936), a translator and novelist. Her 1891 serial (and then book) called *Nisvan-ı İslam* (Women of Islam) modelled the articulate, educated Ottoman woman by staging a series of conversations with European female visitors to the elite home (the 'harem visit'). But increasingly, published female writers were the upper-middle-stratum graduates of Ottoman state schools (like Sa'iba and her aunt).[18]

[16] F. M. M., 'The Bridge of Galata', in Mrs Max Müller, *Letters from Constantinople* (London: Longmans, Green, and Co., 1897), 10–22; 20.

[17] Elizabeth B. Frierson, 'Unimagined Communities: Women and Education in the Late-Ottoman Empire, 1876–1909', *Critical Matrix* 9: 2 (1995), 55–90.

[18] Frierson observes: 'Perhaps what changed in the 1890s was that reading and writing were suddenly enough, that money and power were not base requirements for a woman to participate in public debates.' Elizabeth B. Frierson, 'Women in Late Ottoman Intellectual History', in Elizabeth Ozdalga (ed.), *Late Ottoman Society: The Intellectual Legacy* (London: Routledge, 2005), 135–61; 137.

Like *Sa'iba*'s dedication, the first issue of the major and long-running Ottoman women's magazine *Hanımlara mahsus gazete* (Ladies' Own Gazette, est. 1895) explicitly praised the sultan for attention to female education. Magazines positioned themselves as tools of further education for school graduates who were now married and based in the home.[19] In the Ottoman women's press—as in equivalent publications in Arabic—the rhetoric of 'rights' focused mostly on education for the purposes of wise motherhood and efficient home-making. Increasingly, though, other ambitions came to the fore as women began to move into professional roles encouraged by institutional expansion. Turkish and Arabic women's magazines indicate that women were aware of parallel developments across Europe. These journals introduced women's voices into public political debate on progress and authority in the Empire.[20] But as historian Madeline Zilfi reminds us, 'The architects of the Tanzimat were committed to a new order and a more inclusive social vision but never to the extent of destroying the elitist, patriarchal character of the social hierarchy.'[21] Indeed, it was through the top-down reforms of this male elite that Ottoman women manoeuvred their own engagements with a new age.[22] We should be careful to see the limits of reform of patriarchal power.

Domestic slavery remained a reality in elite Ottoman households—as we see in *Sa'iba*—until the beginning of the twentieth century, even though the Ottoman slave trade as an international operation was ended in 1877 and the Istanbul slave market had been closed in 1846. Slavery continued covertly even as manumission grew. Freed slaves sometimes remained in service in families who had purchased them, often as children (as is described for Marjana, in Sa'iba's natal household). The large harems of the *haute-elite* became famous among Europeans (and were a focus in Orientalist art and memoirs); but middle-class families often had only one or two servitors. Zilfi observes: 'Popular and historical accounts recall female slaves primarily in male-centred terms', 'as the concubines or potential concubines of male family members. Yet most female slaves spent

[19] Ibid. 148.

[20] Frierson, 'Women' and 'Unimagined Communities'; Hülya Yıldız, 'Rethinking the Political: Ottoman Women as Feminist Subjects', *Journal of Gender Studies* 27: 2 (2018), 177–91.

[21] Zilfi, *Women and Slavery*, 234.

[22] Frierson, 'Unimagined Communities'.

most of their time with other women. Female slaves from toddlers to pensioners served as companions, servants, and often the personal property of the women of the home.'[23]

Even as there were calls for complete abolition, some Ottoman writers defended slavery as a kind of benevolent, paternalistic institution, citing the 'kin-like' relations between masters/mistresses and their domestic slaves. Even certain reformers who decried the practice had slaves at home.[24] Some Western observers followed the lead of Ottoman commentators in distinguishing Ottoman slavery from other institutional histories of slavery. But a slave or ex-slave was never a true member of the family, and other observers recognized the underlying violence and cruelty of enslavement. Artist and travel writer Mary Adelaide Walker (1820–1905), resident in Istanbul for nearly thirty years, attempted a 'balanced' explanation of the Ottoman slavery institution particularly regarding female slaves in *Eastern Life and Scenery with Excursions in Asia Minor, Mytilene, Crete and Roumania* (1886). She noted 'benevolent' aspects but did not neglect to observe that Ottoman slavery was as violent, coercive, and inhumane as any other institutionalized enslavement.

These institutions—old and new—are part of al-Bustani's story. Though *Sa'iba*'s rendering of Istanbul social spaces is sketchy at times—there's no evidence that the author ever went there—the novel utilizes the contours of this moment in the Ottoman Empire, and its spatial correlates, as its characters move through the city—to schools, shops, military barracks, and a clandestine gambling den. The novel's spatial descriptions evoke changes in the administrative, educational, entertainment, and residential make-up of the city.

The city's official heart had been old 'Astana' (Istanbul), famous for its skyline punctuated by minarets and domes. The women who open the novel probably shop in the old central district. The nearby old neighbourhood of Fatih traditionally housed some of the characters'

[23] Zilfi, *Women and Slavery*, 155. The complex topic of slavery within Muslim-majority societies—and the generally racially marked differential status of European-origin versus African-origin slaves—has been much written about. See the Select Bibliography for reading suggestions.

[24] Zilfi, *Women and Slavery*, 229, giving as an example the high bureaucrat Midhat Pasha: 'a progressive... an advocate for girls' education, he gave and received gifts of slaves even while proclaiming distaste for the institution.' 'His real Jeffersonian moment... is reflected in his purchase of a *cariye* [Arab. *jariya*] to become his second wife.'

extended family. The Sublime Porte (Arab. *Al-bab al-'ali*) referred in the first instance to the palace and seat of rule of the reigning sultan and his regime. The earlier centre of rule was the Topkapı Palace located at the eastern tip of the Istanbul peninsula where the Sea of Marmara led into the Bosphorus to the north-east and the Golden Horn to the north-west, waterways trisecting the urban space. The sultans of the nineteenth century moved their headquarters across the waters to the rapidly developing and somewhat Europeanized area around and beyond Galata, first to the Dolmabahçe Palace on the Bosphorus (1856) and then, from the 1880s, to Abdülhamid II's newly built Yıldız complex with its many structures and gardens, further along the Bosphorus shore. This spurred residential development in the area as well as construction of government premises such as the barracks to which Lutfi goes.[25] The central Imperial administration remained based in the older city: the offices of the Grand Vizier, the Minister of Foreign Affairs, and the Council of State.

The cityscape these characters inhabit also speaks to emerging presences. Farid's preferred area of the city is Beyoğlu. Also known by its Europeanized name as Pera, this area on the Asian side of the city sat on rising ground to the north of the old walled town of Galata. It became the heart of Istanbul's 'European' quarter. Entertainment venues, European-style hotels, and financial institutions were clustered along and around the Grande Rue de Pera, and the architecture echoed European modernism.[26] The area was also the quintessential 'tourist trap'. Fatma Aliye described it acerbically:

> the Europeans, upon arriving in Dersaadet [Abode of Felicity: Istanbul], descend directly to the Beyoğlu hotels. . . . the translator-guides whom they keep by their side don't even know anything other than the world of Beyoğlu, and so they just make something up and say whatever comes into their heads. . . . The travellers, believing the things they have heard from them are true, add them to their travel accounts. And when we read some of these travel accounts, we think some country unknown to us is being discussed.[27]

[25] For description of these developments see Zeynep Çelik, *The Remaking of Istanbul: Portrait of an Ottoman City in the Nineteenth Century* (Seattle: University of Washington Press, 1986).

[26] Ibid. 132–4.

[27] Translated in Marilyn Booth and Holly Shissler, 'Fatma Aliye's *Nisvan-ı Islam:* Istanbul, Paris, Beirut, Cairo, 1891–96', in Marilyn Booth and Claire Savina (eds.), *Ottoman Translations: Circulating Texts from Bombay to Paris* (Edinburgh: Edinburgh University Press, 2023), 327–88; 334.

In the prolific reformist journalist and novelist Ahmet Midhat's (1844–1912) 1890/91 novel *Müşahedat*, the educated female Armenian women 'are orphans whose roots extend into the sordid depths of Beyoğlu, the "other" Istanbul, infidel and European, the Istanbul of minorities and foreigners'.[28]

When the narrator of *Sa'iba* 'ushers' the reader 'after asking your permission . . . inside a home tucked away in a corner of Beyoğlu', it is not surprising to find a theatre stage, behind which is concealed a gambling parlour where Boulos and Farid make their plans. The theatrical setting seems appropriate: the novel stages its layers of deception to remind the reader that nothing is as it seems, in this slippery new world of 'modernity' represented by Beyoğlu.

Although Istanbul-centred, the novel displays a larger social and political canvas, as it draws on challenges provincial Ottoman cities faced, some of which would have been familiar to al-Bustani's Arabophone readers in Ottoman Syria. Sa'iba's father had been posted to the European-Ottoman city of Salonica; in the novel, Lutfi seeks a posting there in hopes of finding a more salubrious clime for his family, physically and emotionally. It is interesting that al-Bustani, from an Arabophone Ottoman province at the east of the Mediterranean, would choose the European end of the Empire as Sa'iba's birthplace and Lutfi's destination. This added verisimilitude and colour to the story, for Salonica was a centre of military activity appropriate to the father's and husband's careers, and a hotbed of clandestine resistance that partly shapes the story's outcome. Moreover, Salonica was particularly cosmopolitan. The site of early experimentation in Ottoman municipal government and urban infrastructural reform, it was an emblem and site of 'modernity', open to myriad influences and models, paralleling al-Bustani's portraits of Sa'iba and her aunt as forward-looking, emphatically Ottoman women.

Salonica was well known to visitors from further west, and the choice of it as a setting might also hint at a desire on the author's part to see her novel translated into a western European language. Perhaps such a desire is also suggested by the narrator's digression in Chapter 3, setting out a schema of differences between 'Eastern' and 'Western' marriage, focusing on 'Eastern' practices. Would Arab readers likely

[28] Carter Vaughn Findley, *Turkey, Islam, Nationalism, and Modernity: A History* (New Haven: Yale University Press, 2010), 186.

to pick up such a novel have needed this didactic interruption? Or was it aimed at other readers? In any case, it assumed a shared if differently practised understanding about modern marriage as companionship and mutual help, but its smooth encapsulation of ideal young marriages sits uneasily with the novel's outcome.

The narrator's explanation of betrothal and marriage as understood by some late nineteenth-century Arab reformists—the man can shape the woman in accord with his tastes and needs—implies that 'companionate' did not mean 'egalitarian'.[29] Companionate marriage remained a patriarchal construct where men retained authority over women—and over what women 'should' be. Companionate marriage was mostly viewed through a male gaze. However, women desired a more equal arrangement, and writers of novels, magazine articles, and biographical sketches tried to visualize other models by invoking both historical examples and their own experiences and hopes.

This didactic passage occurs as the couple who have chosen each other are getting married. As historian Fruma Zachs has noted, *Sa'iba* is unusual amongst early Arabic novels in being set mostly after the wedding rather than closing with a wedding as the presumed 'happy ending' that resolves the heroine's dilemma and brings her home.[30] This is a mark of Alis al-Bustani's perspicacity in diagnosing limitations to 'modern' changes swirling around her world. Perhaps it aligns her novel with 1890s New Woman Fiction in Britain—and sensation fiction of the 1860s. Lyn Pykett observes this fiction 'exploring the contradictions in the dominant ideology of the feminine ... [and thus]

[29] In her study of Alis's mother Rahil, Lindner sees Rahil and Butrus's marriage as based on 'successful egalitarian relations' and links this to Butrus al-Bustani's important 1849 speech on female education (Lindner, 'Rahil', 64–5). However, in that speech—as in Alis's description of betrothal practices—different domains of activity are spelled out and the female spouse is 'helpmeet'. Of course, Butrus may have believed—but did not say in the speech—that such relations went both ways. In her article on this speech, Zachs notes Butrus al-Bustani's notion—which would become widespread—of men's and women's 'complementary' roles; women's rights 'were interpreted as women's duties to men'. But she reminds us that for this early moment, the speech was 'unprecedented' in calling for 'a kind of social equality' (Fruma Zachs, 'Feminism for Men: A Note on Butrus al-Bustani's Lecture on the Education of Women (1849)', in Adel Beshara (ed.), *Butrus al-Bustani: Spirit of the Age* (Melbourne: IPhoenix Publishing, 2014), 113–30; 127, 129). In my view, the speech also diverges from other early (and much later) statements supporting female education by suggesting that women's and girls' own intellectual aspirations are important—though these are folded into a domestic female role.

[30] Zachs, 'Subversive Voices', 345, 349–50. This essay was the first, to my knowledge, to assess this novel's importance. Zachs and I agree on many points.

focused on marriage rather than on the courtship which formed the main narrative trajectory of most Victorian fiction'.[31]

When she wrote and published her novel, Alis al-Bustani was unmarried. But she had a nuanced understanding of how a modernized patriarchy worked. When the new model of marriage goes wrong—in this case, because the male partner cannot take 'companionate' to its logical fulfilment of listening and trust—the result is tragedy. Sa'iba's husband remains unable to believe in her probity. In this patriarchal system in rapid transition, men wanted 'modern' wives but were not themselves updated into new sets of expectations. Even the 'good man', Lutfi, cannot believe in his wife's innocence when the ruses of other men seem to put the idea in doubt.

Alis al-Bustani was not the only nineteenth-century Arabophone female writer who questioned the viability of this arrangement for women, but *Sa'iba* is particularly attentive to the limitations to 'new' patterns, both strategies and beliefs. Foreshadowing the story's denouement, the excursus on 'Eastern' versus 'Western' marriage exposes the ideological justifications of 'honour' as a discourse of protection aimed at females—a precarious 'protection' indeed. Sa'iba tries to preserve her own honour.

Geography and politics are intertwined with family drama, the personal story with the fortunes of the Ottoman state. Lutfi is posted to Salonica Governorate to take charge of public security in a provincial town. Incidents of theft and violence are intensifying. In this period, criminal gangs might shade into political oppositional forces. (Later, in 1909—eighteen years after the novel was published—Salonica city was the centre of the political movement for regime change known as the Young Turks.[32])

[31] Lyn Pykett, *The 'Improper' Feminine: The Women's Sensation Novel and the New Woman Writing* (London: Routledge, 1992), 6, quoted in Nora Gilbert, *Gone Girls, 1684–1901: Flights of Feminist Resistance in the Eighteenth- and Nineteenth-Century British Novel* (Oxford: Oxford University Press, 2023), 173.

[32] Deposed, Abdülhamid II was exiled to Salonica and resided in a mansion built by a historically prominent Salonica family of the city's large Jewish community. On Salonica's history, communal make-up, and political roles see Mark Mazower, *Salonica, City of Ghosts: Christians, Muslims and Jews 1430–1950* (London: Harper Perennial, 2004); Méropi Anastassiodou-Dumont, *Salonique, 1830–1912. Une ville ottomane à l'âge des Réformes* (Leiden: Brill, 1997); Basil C. Gounaris, 'Salonica', *Review* (Fernand Braudel Center), special issue, 'Port-Cities of the Eastern Mediterranean 1800–1914', 16, no. 4 (Fall 1993), 499–518. A novel by another early female writer was set in Salonica and published as these events were occurring: Farida 'Atiya's *Hasna' Salonik* (*The Belle of Salonica*, 1909).

Lutfi and his detachment begin to stabilize the situation. But neither the state nor the marriage is secure: both are fragile faced with corrupt internal forces that reach into the household. The anonymous letters to Lutfi that erode his trust in his wife arrive at his military HQ as well as at home. Moral corruption, insecurity, and greed undermine both the home and the state. Gender ideology is central to this internal rot.

The implied parallel between the state and patriarchal masculinity does not mean this novel is a political allegory. Rather, it asks the question if new concepts of womanhood, and women's new aspirations, can thrive when attitudes, practices, and institutions continue to privilege those born male. Farid believes that Lutfi's existence is the only obstacle between him and Sa'iba: he cannot see her as an individual with her own will, but only as a commodity available to the highest (male) bidder. Although Lutfi does not share this outlook, he, too, is shaped by masculinist presuppositions; he finds it difficult to believe in his wife even though he wants—and struggles—to do so. Persistent notions linking family 'honour' and (always-suspect) female behaviour are too strong. *Sa'iba* attends to the darker side of what can happen when modern men—Lutfi as well as Farid—remain governed by ideas about gender privilege and gendered 'nature'. The novel's ending delivers the forceful message that when 'honour' is at stake, women pay the highest price. The novel dramatizes its message by recourse to motifs that nineteenth-century readers in Europe would have recognized as the province of the Gothic novel.

A Victorian Novel?

French literature was by far the best known (and most translated) European literary tradition among Alis al-Bustani's educated peers. But *Sa'iba*, in its formal divergences from other Arabic fiction of the era, suggests an acquaintance with the English novel (with which the writer was probably familiar through her education and her family). The marriage plot was common to fiction in both languages, as was the focus on young women who struggle to rise above painful circumstances, to maintain their bodily and social integrity, and to strive for a satisfying life.

Sa'iba displays experimentation with motifs common to the Gothic strain in Anglophone fiction (the novelist's sister, nearly thirty years before, may have drawn from the narrative modes of English-language sensation novels).[33] Emerging as a sensibility in novels and poetry from the mid-1700s, becoming wildly popular with the spectacular 1790s novels of Ann Radcliffe (1764–1823), Gothic may be understood as a mode or mood more than a genre: a cluster of motifs, themes, and emphases that has maintained a purchase on imaginative literature (and other artistic forms) across the world. 'Classic' Gothic combined an emphasis on affect and emotional intensity with tellingly atmospheric landscape, an architecture that allows or encourages confinement to the point of incarceration, and elements of the supernatural. It became a vehicle for exploring female subordination—tactics and effects—through presenting female characters as subject to machinations of family members and suitors. By the mid-Victorian period, the focus of these works had shifted from the more exotic scenery of Radcliffe's imaginary Italy to urban Britain; and from the space of the forbidding castle as prison—the quintessential Gothic setting—to familiar domestic middle-class spaces. Home, the message seemed to be, was not a safe space—a theme we find in *Sa'iba*.[34] In parallel, the exteriorized terrors of earlier Gothic moved to a focus on the dark corners of the human psyche. Emotions of melancholy, despair, and outright fear became inevitable accompaniments to 'love' in a context of patriarchal power relations.

This literary history was not unknown to Arabophone readers. Zaynab Fawwaz's mid-1890s Arabic biographical dictionary of notable women had an entry on Ann Radcliffe that recognized Gothic's expression of heightened emotion, reliance on a sense of the supernatural, and envisioned impact on readers:

> She concerned herself with writing stories in a new style and swiftly became famous for her dexterity at composition and eloquence. Above all, these stories projected intense emotional reactions, such as dread and awe, and highlighted obscure secrets and strange phenomena, leading readers to

[33] Ghenwa Hayek, 'Experimental Female Fictions; Or, the Brief Wondrous Life of the Naha Sensation Story', *Middle Eastern Literatures* 16: 3 (2013), 249–65.

[34] Alexandra Warwick, 'Victorian Gothic', in Catherine Spooner and Emma McEvoy (eds.), *The Routledge Companion to Gothic* (London and New York: Routledge, 2007), 29–37. In the same volume, see Alison Milbank, 'Gothic Femininities', 155–63. Amongst the copious scholarship on the Gothic, see also Carol Margaret Davison, *Gothic Literature 1764–1824* (Cardiff: University of Wales Press, 2009).

imagine themselves surrounded by apparitions, conjured shadows, spirits both hellish and divine. And then, the secret emerges, revealed at the story's end as having a natural explanation. It is said she herself imagined such phantasms. Imprinted on her mind, they led her to mental imbalance at life's end.[35]

Translations and adaptations of European novels with Gothic elements existed in Arabic, and Ottoman Turkish fiction—in particular, novels by the prolific writer and journalist Ahmet Midhat—drew on Gothic motifs and themes.[36] Moreover, this was not a completely 'imported' sensibility: the copious indigenous fund of stories, drawing from Arabic, Persian, Turkish, and Indian wellsprings, could make 'European' Gothic sound familiar, even as Nahda and later intellectuals decried the 'irrational' elements of what they labelled 'superstition' or 'fancy' (as they associated this with 'uneducated women'). Some early twentieth-century Egyptian male novelists even used supernatural motifs as they warned against what they saw as deviant social behaviour inimical to a rational bourgeois world.[37] But if we consider novels by women, and novels before the twentieth century, the picture looks different. In *Sa'iba*, such 'hauntings' are not separate from an intellectualized bourgeois consciousness but are part of it as long as old ideas about gender persist—specifically, suspicions about women's sexual integrity.[38] Radcliffe focused her Gothic

[35] 'Rad klif mu'allifa inkiliziyya', in Zaynab Fawwaz al-'Amili, *al-Durr al-manthur fi tabaqat rabbat al-khudur* (Cairo Bulaq: al-Matba'a al-kubra al-amiriyya, 1312 [1894/5]), 198. On this work, see Marilyn Booth, *Classes of Ladies of Cloistered Spaces: Writing Feminist History through Biography in Fin-de-Siècle Egypt* (Edinburgh: Edinburgh University Press, 2015).

[36] A. Holly Shissler, 'Haunting Ottoman Middle-Class Sensibility: Ahmet Midhat Efendi's Gothic', in Marilyn Booth (ed.), *Migrating Texts: Circulating Translations around the Ottoman Mediterranean* (Edinburgh: Edinburgh University Press, 2019), 193–209. Others have placed 'Gothic' in early republican Turkey and early twentieth-century Egypt. See Tuğçe Biçakçı Syed, ch. 3, 'Gothicizing the Ottoman Past and Building Modern Turkey in Turkish Gothic Novels of the 1920s', in Karen Grumberg (ed.), *Middle Eastern Gothics: Literature, Spectral Modernities, and the Restless Past* (Cardiff: University of Wales Press, 2022), 81–107; in the same volume, Alexandra Shraytekh (Chreiteh), 'Efendi Gothic: A Forgotten Prehistory of the Arabic Novel', 133–63.

[37] Chreiteh, 'Efendi Gothic'.

[38] In the Radcliffian novel, Nora Gilbert comments, 'Women may be wrong to fear ghosts and goblins, Radcliffe seems to be saying, but their fear of patriarchal tyranny is always fully founded' (Nora Gilbert, *Gone Girls, 1684–1901: Flights of Feminist Resistance in the Eighteenth- and Nineteenth-Century British Novel* (Oxford: Oxford University Press, 2023), 74).

lens on women as categorical targets of persecution, entrapment, and masculine prerogative, helping to set a literary trajectory that spoke to complicated societal shifts which displaced or re-placed men and women occupationally and economically, spatially and legally, with profound ramifications for social relations. In this sense *Sa'iba* is strongly linked to the British Gothic tradition.

At the outset of our novel, there is no sign of Gothic haunting. We are in a modern, prosperous world capital, Istanbul of the late Ottoman Empire, and the characters we meet inhabit bright quarters in the administrative, commercial, and elite residential precincts—old and new—of the city. But even as we accompany Fahima and Saniyya on their post-shopping boat excursion, the atmosphere takes a darker turn. Leaving the house, Fahima exclaims over 'the fine prospect that Nature supplies'; but as the women gaze shoreward from the water and Fahima relates the background to her niece's impending wedding, '[t]he atmosphere was turbid, the sky overcast with heavy but patchy scattered clouds that cast a curtain of shadow rolling across the water and darkening the surface' (Chapter 1). Clouds 'deflect the sun's heavy heat' but they also presage a 'cloudy' story. There will be intimations of ghosts in *Sa'iba*: these are the 'clouds' of persistent beliefs about 'women's nature'.

For, after the joyous wedding, and although this is a chosen, 'companionate' marriage, we soon see signs of missed communication. The clouds are not only external. In Chapter 3, Sa'iba's companion (and milk-sister, for they were nursed by the same mother) sings a prescient song: a warning of love's trials, which 'waste away' the individual. Sa'iba and Lutfi may have a companionate relationship where each listens to the other, but their effusions are laced with foreboding. The song is doubly revelatory: of Sa'iba's trajectory and of Sorayya's hidden emotions. These are framed within an assumption voiced by Lutfi. Which of the two of them—Sa'iba or Lutfi—would be 'the stronger' sacrificial figure, if their love demanded it? Lutfi assumes that it would be him: that being protected is the unquestionable lot of the cherished female, while physical and moral strength belong to the male. The story proves him wrong. Neither Farid nor Lutfi is a patriarchal tyrant and one strength of the novel is that the male characters—even selfish, hapless Farid—may draw readers' sympathies, as we see masculinities in crisis—even (or especially?) if the men don't recognize it.

Victorian Gothic's focus on the spaces of urban bourgeois life is pertinent here. Gothic tropes emerge at the edges of Istanbul, the modern city, and in the state employee's own home. These tropes intersect with intimations of haunting. The first unsafe space is the rooftop veranda of a hunters' lodge concealed in the forest edging the city—a correlate of the isolated Gothic castle. It is both 'outside' and 'of' the city, a refuge for men seeking a leisure break from urban stresses. The second Gothic space is Sa'iba's own garden. In Arabic and Turkish literature, the garden had long been an ideal space of beauty and conviviality, and a spiritual haven. While it is Sa'iba's space of solace—and where she and her husband have their conversations on love and life—it is also a space of vulnerability, invasion, and violence. The Gothic as situated in familiar urban spaces introduces the permeability of the elite home to criminality and violence.[39]

The characters who inhabit these spaces are subject to unease and fear, represented as a series of hauntings. Reading in the garden, Sa'iba voices what Lutfi has already recalled hearing: her feelings of despondency. Although she misses Lutfi when he is at work, is this all that is going on? She has an uncanny dream. She senses herself pulled to (and by) an unknown force, an unfamiliar voice calling out to her, a secret that eludes her. Of course, the 'secret' impossible to uncover comprises the sinister machinations of Boulos, Marjana, and Farid to separate Sa'iba and Lutfi. There is nothing supernatural here; the uncanny is fully human. That Sa'iba relates her misgivings in a site of seclusion gives the private garden setting a perfect Gothic gloss.

With the scene at the hunting lodge just outside the city (Chapter 7), Gothic elements come to the fore. Here is the remote and isolated, possibly forbidding—yet completely modern—'castle' of this story—as mentioned, a male preserve. ('Hunters were in the habit of gathering there in the early afternoon hours to sleep through the worst heat of the day.') Young Farid becomes the evil abductor, even if, somewhat clueless, he is simply following his wily 'mentor' Boulos's instructions. But Sa'iba is not a gullible object of the Gothic gaze. (And Farid's status as villain is also modulated by the portrait we get, as he waits, of a young man unsure of himself, despite his surface arrogance. Even his stylish appearance is not quite as he would wish.)

[39] As in Alis's sister Idlid's earlier short fiction, 'Henry and Amelia', analysed by Hayek, 'Experimental Female Fictions'.

Sa'iba and Farid's dramatic stand-off on the lodge's rooftop terrace finds Farid pressing his cousin for an answer to his desire to have her, and Sa'iba pressing closer to the open edge of the rooftop terrace, overlooking the rocky basin below, and threatening to kill herself. Having locked the door to the terrace, incarcerating Sa'iba, Farid's actions fill out the Gothicized space of terror. The site itself becomes a character, a counterpart to Sa'iba's inner turmoil: 'She felt as though the floor was trembling...'.

When Sa'iba manages to escape from this 'fortress', the affective contagion of fear and mistrust merely spreads: her concealed husband, brought to the forest surrounding the lodge by another anonymous letter, catches sight of her. At home, the emotional temperature is at fever-height, mirrored in Sa'iba's and Lutfi's physical states—and the bodily harms that infect them. Feeling alienated from his marriage, Lutfi travels alone to his new posting. Moving through the Salonican countryside (Chapter 10), he finds the wild and dark natural scene to be a correlative of his internal melancholy—or worse. Like Sa'iba with her dream, recounted in the garden, Lutfi encounters the supernatural in his own encounter with nature: the presence of a hidden, mysterious power in an obscuring darkness, a mysterious figure just beyond reach. The Gothic victim is not only the female. Lutfi is equally a victim of social expectations, although (like Farid) he is in a position to make decisions that women cannot access. Lutfi himself becomes a supernatural image with which female characters must contend. Sa'iba's companion Sorayya, too, faces a mysterious force beyond herself as she sits alone in her room. (In contrast Boulos's shadow-opponent at cards, in the gambling den, is both hilarious and woeful, in what is possibly a mockery of Gothic tropes.)

Gothic novels may include an irruption into the present of a past that refuses to be (or remain) buried—history itself as a haunting. In *Sa'iba*, that 'past' is the institution of arranged marriage between cousins, which Farid assumes as his right. The weight of the past is also in the accumulation of attitudes that have conditioned Lutfi into an inability to trust Sa'iba on the basis of her word.

If *Sa'iba* portrays imbalance in this modern conjugal relationship—and shows this slice of modernity as one that reifies strictly gendered spheres of occupation—the novel also shows the vulnerability and pain that both Sa'iba and Lutfi experience. But Sa'iba knows that, ultimately, she is defenceless—as she thinks, locked on the hunting lodge terrace, about how this situation will look to her husband should he find out. As Carol Davison has observed, 'transgressive threshold crossings are a vital feature of the Gothic genre'.[40] Sa'iba's is not 'transgressive'—she left home and went to the lodge because she received word that her husband was in danger—but her peers are likely to see her that way. But family 'honour' is a threshold of sorts which Sa'iba knows rests upon her reputation, governed by her movements through space rather than by her own sense of probity. Sa'iba is emphatically not the rebellious heroine of so much nineteenth-century British fiction; and this perhaps makes her story all the more poignant.

A European Intertext

> His work obligations completed, he hired a small boat to take him home. He mounted the steps from the landing and nearly ran to the garden gate. He yanked it open. There he saw Sa'iba, sitting under the willow tree, reading. Tears flowed down her face. He went over to her and asked what it was that had made her cry. (Chapter 5)

Sa'iba is reading 'the tale of Geneviève' de Brabant, in this passage quoted above, a medieval French noblewoman sometimes regarded as a Christian saint though never canonized. Geneviève's tale made her a quasi-legendary figure. Geneviève featured as an entry in the encyclopaedia originated by Alis's father, despite his aversion to figures whose historical provenance was questionable. Butrus involved family members in his projects. It is not far-fetched to wonder whether female Bustanis contributed some of the many entries on famous females in history and myth. (See Appendix 2.)

Lutfi finds his spouse crying over a tale of a woman's rejection by her absent husband after a jealous rival sows doubt about her probity, knowing how easily women can become suspect. Lutfi recognizes that he ought not to follow this ancient pattern (and al-Bustani's inserted European storyline suggests it's an issue transcending time and place).

Al-Bustani's weeping heroine simply mentions the tale without elaborating its contents (in a novel containing a fair amount of explication). This suggests she assumed the tale was familiar to her Arabic readers and to Turkish readers in the novel: Sa'iba's husband clearly

[40] Davison, *Gothic Literature 1764–1824*, 31.

knows the story. There are parallels large and small between our novel and the tale, as there are Gothic motifs aplenty in both. That this Arabic Ottoman Victorian Gothic novel draws on a Latin-German-French legend familiar to its Istanbul-based characters to foreshadow its narrative arc and emphasize its message reminds us of nineteenth-century literature's global reach.

* * *

What did Sa'iba, as character, represent for Alis al-Bustani and her peers, young women living—and reading—in a time of change? They probably perceived exciting and realizable possibilities as well as troubling deterrents. Sa'iba is the wise, determined, and vocal daughter; she is the accommodating yet intellectually independent companion-spouse; and she is a sensitive reader of narratives and character. *Sa'iba* confronts issues that worried young women and men, and their elders: women's ability to resist arranged marriages; the waning of the gender-segregation system; girls' education; and 'corrupt' pursuits of male youth. The novel represents a woman-centred Nahda, a space in which women (and men) debated what 'freedom' means.

Sa'iba also casts doubt on the novel as a morally educative force. 'Good behaviour' is not always rewarded; 'good men', if they retain masculinist predilections, are not good enough. Lutfi fulfils the requirements that female writers posited as ideal modern masculinity. He is sensitive to his wife's feelings, appreciates her learning, is socially and fiscally responsible, and has personal integrity. But, even Lutfi cannot escape the hold of historically sedimented concepts of femininity. Above all, *Sa'iba* offers a devastating portrait of the limits to 'reform' posed by persistent patriarchal attitudes safeguarded by norms of 'honour'—sometimes fatally so for those born female.

NOTE ON THE TEXT, TRANSLATION, AND TRANSLITERATION

Sa'iba was published in 1891 by al-Maktaba al-Adabiyya (Literary Library/Bookshop) in Beirut—although on the title page, it is al-Matba'a al-Adabiyya, the Literary Press, that appears. This press was associated with a major Beirut newspaper of the time, *Lisan al-hal* (The Spokesperson, established 1876/7 as a semi-weekly; it became a daily in 1895). The founder-editor of both was Khalil Sarkis (1842–1915), who was married to Alis's older sister Louisa (1853–1923). (Their eldest sister, Adelaide (1849–1933), was married to Amin Sarkis (1845–96), brother of Khalil.) As a young man, Khalil had collaborated with Alis's father Butrus in opening a press and bookshop. According to historian of the Arabic press Ami Ayalon, Khalil initiated *Lisan al-hal* as a 'business mainstay' to underwrite the press and, Ayalon comments, he embodied a key strategy in early Arabic publishing, 'the printer as publisher... at once assimilating a new product and creating the market for it'.[1] The still-new genre of the novel was important to this enterprise.

The book was printed, we are told on the title page, 'with a license from the esteemed Ministry of Education, number 1535/817'. This must refer to the Ottoman Ministry of Public Education instituted in 1857. Such was standard practice; but it may also signal the Ministry's tacit approval (or the author and publishers' wish for that approval) of the book's possible use as a teaching text in Arabic/Ottoman state girls' schools. The heavy emphasis in the novel on the benefits of schooling would be consonant with this goal.

To my knowledge, the novel was never republished. A new edition is to come out with the American University in Beirut Press, edited and introduced by Dr Rana Issa.

I have sought a translation style that echoes the novel's creative partnership with Victorian fiction. In that context, one might render the novel's title as 'Sa'iba; or, Verity', proposing an English feminine

[1] Ami Ayalon, *The Arabic Print Revolution: Cultural Production and Mass Readership* (Cambridge: Cambridge University Press, 2016), 41, 43.

name that is a period-appropriate near equivalent to 'Sa'iba', although I use the original Arabic name throughout the story.

Naming practices posed a conundrum. As the Introduction proposes, this novel is at once an Arabic novel, an Ottoman novel, and a Victorian novel. Set at the political centre of the late Ottoman Empire, the characters are implied to be of Turkish rather than Arab origin, and to be Turkish speakers. Then, shouldn't their given names be transliterated according to Ottoman Turkish rather than Arabic conventions? Saebe rather than Sa'iba? Furthermore, this Arabic-origin active participle meaning 'correct' or 'apposite' or 'perfectly aimed' is not a common given name in Arabic, but it is attested in Turkish.[2] Yet the novel's origins are Arabic and I have elected to spell the names phonetically as they are spelled and spoken in Arabic rather than as they would be transliterated in modern Turkish as Ottoman Turkish names (thus: Lutfi and not Lütfi; Soraya (or Sorayya) and not Süreyya (or the classical Arabic Thurayyā')), and so forth. Pronunciation of these names in Turkish would be close though not identical to their pronunciation in Levant Arabic.

However, for Turkish titles and institutions, I have retained a 'more Turkish' spelling, as we are, after all, with these characters in Istanbul. In the Arabic, the elite male title 'Bey' is spelled *bek* but I have used Bey, reflecting oral pronunciation in both Turkish and Arabic; Defterdar for the Arabic *daftardar*; the famous Istanbul school for orphans Darüşşafaka, spelled in Arabic as *dar al-shafaqa*. Because phonetic spelling would ease the reader's pronunciation, I have used the Arabic *j* rather than the Turkish *c* (both pronounced as *j*): thus, *jariya* (Arabic) instead of *cariye* (Turkish); *farajiyya* (Arabic) rather than *ferace* (Turkish). I have altered *yashmaq* (Arabic)/*yaşmak* (Turkish) to *yashmak*. Working between two languages—in fictional settings that exemplify the polyglot complexity of the Ottoman world—I have made compromises that I hope are congenial rather than confusing.

[2] Arif Hikmet Par, *A'dan Z'ye Ansiklopedik Türk Adları ve Soyadları Sözlüğü*, s.v. 'Saib—Saibe' (Istanbul, 1981). (The male name is also spelt 'Saip'.) I am indebted to Johann Strauss for this reference.

SELECT BIBLIOGRAPHY

Early Arabic fiction, women writers, gender debates, and the Nahda (see also the section 'The Bustani family and their writings')

Ashour, Radwa, Ferial Ghazoul, and Hasna Reda-Mekdashi (eds.), *Arab Women Writers: A Critical Reference Guide, 1873–1999*, trans. Mandy McClure (Cairo: American University in Cairo Press, 2008).

Ayalon, Ami, *The Arabic Print Revolution: Cultural Production and Mass Readership* (Cambridge: Cambridge University Press, 2016).

Badran, Margot, *Feminists, Islam, and Nation: Gender and the Making of Modern Egypt* (Princeton: Princeton University Press, 1995).

Baron, Beth, *The Women's Awakening in Egypt: Culture, Society and the Press* (New Haven: Yale University Press, 1994).

Booth, Marilyn, *The Career and Communities of Zaynab Fawwaz: Feminist Thinking in* Fin-de-siècle *Egypt* (Oxford: Oxford University Press, 2021).

Booth, Marilyn, 'Women and the Emergence of the Arabic Novel', in Wa'il Hassan (ed.), *The Oxford Handbook of Arab Novelistic Traditions* (Oxford: Oxford University Press, 2017), 135–53.

Booth, Marilyn, 'Liberal Thought and the "Problem" of Women', in Jens Hanssen and Max Weiss (eds.), *Arabic Thought beyond the Liberal Age: Towards an Intellectual History of the Nahda* (Cambridge: Cambridge University Press, 2016), 187–213.

Booth, Marilyn, *May Her Likes Be Multiplied: Biography and Gender Politics in Egypt* (Berkeley and Los Angeles: University of California Press, 2001).

Booth, Marilyn, 'Peripheral Visions: Translational Polemics and Feminist Arguments in Colonial Egypt', in Anna Ball and Karim Mattar (eds.), *Edinburgh Companion to the Postcolonial Middle East* (Edinburgh: Edinburgh University Press, 2018), 183–212.

Cuno, Kenneth M., *Modernising Marriage: Family, Ideology, and Law in Nineteenth and Early Twentieth Century Egypt* (Syracuse: Syracuse University Press, 2015).

El-Ariss, Tarek (ed.), *The Arab Renaissance: A Bilingual Anthology of the Nahda* (New York: Modern Languages Association, Texts and Translations Series, 2018).

Elsadda, Hoda, *Gender, Nation, and the Arabic Novel: Egypt, 1892–2008* (Edinburgh: Edinburgh University Press, 2012).

Hill, Peter, *Utopia and Civilisation in the Arab Nahda* (Cambridge: Cambridge University Press, 2019).

Holt, Elizabeth M., *Fictitious Capital: Silk, Cotton, and the Rise of the Arabic Novel* (New York: Fordham University Press, 2017).

Johnson, Rebecca C., *Stranger Fictions: A History of the Novel in Arabic Translation* (Ithaca: Cornell University Press, 2020).

Patel, Abdulrazzak, *The Arab* Nahdah: *The Making of the Intellectual and Humanist Movement* (Edinburgh: Edinburgh University Press, 2013).

Selim, Samah, *Popular Fiction, Translation and the Nahda in Egypt* (Cham, Switzerland: Palgrave, 2019).

Zeidan, Joseph, *Arab Women Novelists: The Formative Years and Beyond* (Binghamton: State University of New York Press, 1995).

Late Ottoman history: urban formations and gender-focused social, intellectual, and literary history

Booth, Marilyn (ed.). *Migrating Texts: Circulating Translations around the Ottoman Mediterranean* (Edinburgh: Edinburgh University Press, 2019).

Booth, Marilyn, and Claire Savina (eds.), *Ottoman Translations: Circulating Texts from Bombay to Paris* (Edinburgh: Edinburgh University Press, 2023).

Çelik, Zeynep, *The Remaking of Istanbul: Portrait of an Ottoman City in the Nineteenth Century* (Seattle: University of Washington Press, 1986).

Faroqhi, Soraya, 'Women in the Ottoman World: Mid-18th to Early 20th Century', in Suad Joseph (ed.), *Encyclopedia of Women in Islamic Cultures*, vol. 1: *Methodologies, Paradigms and Sources* (Leiden: Brill, 2003), 153–63.

Findley, Carter Vaughn, *Turkey, Islam, Nationalism, and Modernity: A History* (New Haven: Yale University Press, 2010).

Frierson, Elizabeth B., 'Unimagined Communities: Women and Education in the Late-Ottoman Empire, 1876–1909', *Critical Matrix* 9: 2 (1995), 55–90.

Frierson, Elizabeth B., 'Women in Late Ottoman Intellectual History', in Elizabeth Ozdalga (ed.), *Late Ottoman Society: The Intellectual Legacy* (London: Routledge, 2005), 135–61.

Ringer, Monica M., and Etienne E. Charrière (eds.), *Ottoman Culture and the Project of Modernity: Reform and Translation in the Tanzimat Novel* (London: I. B. Tauris, 2020).

Strauss, Johann, 'Who read what in the Ottoman Empire (19th–20th Centuries)?', *Middle Eastern Literatures* 6: 1 (2003), 39–76.

Late Ottoman slavery

Erdem, Y. Hakan, *Slavery in the Ottoman Empire and its Demise, 1800–1909* (Basingstoke: Macmillan and St Antony's College, 1996).

Peirce, Leslie, *A Spectrum of Unfreedom: Captives and Slaves in the Ottoman Empire* (Budapest: Central European University Press (The Natalie Zemon Davis Annual Lectures Series), 2021).

Toledano, Ehud R., *Slavery and Abolition in the Ottoman Middle East* (Seattle: University of Washington Press, 1998).

Zilfi, M. C., 'Servants, Slaves, and the Domestic Order in the Ottoman Middle East', *Hawwa* 2:1 (2004), 1–33.

Zilfi, Madeline C., 'Slavery: The Ottoman Empire', in Suad Joseph (gen. ed.), *Encyclopedia of Women in Islamic Cultures*, vol. 4: *Economics, Education, Mobility and Space* (Leiden: Brill, 2007), 508–10.

Zilfi, Madeline C., *Women and Slavery in the Late Ottoman Empire: The Design of Difference* (Cambridge: Cambridge University Press, 2010).

The al-Bustani family and their writings

Beshara, Adel (ed.), *Butrus al-Bustani: Spirit of the Age* (Melbourne: IPhoenix Publishing, 2014).

Booth, Marilyn, *Classes of Ladies of Cloistered Spaces: Writing Feminist History through Biography in Fin-de-Siècle Egypt* (Edinburgh: Edinburgh University Press, 2015), ch. 6 (on *Da'irat al-ma'arif*).

Booth, Marilyn, '"She herself was the ultimate rule": Arab Women's Biographies of their Missionary Teachers', special issue: 'Missionary Transformations', ed. Eleanor Doumato, *Islam and Christian–Muslim Relations* 13: 4 (Oct. 2002), 427–48.

Al-Bustani, Butrus, *The Clarion of Syria: A Patriot's Call against the Civil War of 1860*, trans. Jens Hanssen and Hicham Safieddine (Berkeley and Los Angeles: University of California Press, 2019).

Al-Bustani, Butrus, 'The Culture of the Arabs Today', from his 1859 'Lecture on the Culture of the Arabs', introduced and translated (with Arabic text) by Stephen Sheehi, in Tarek El-Ariss (ed.), *The Arab Renaissance: A Bilingual Anthology of the Nahda* (New York: Modern Languages Association, Texts and Translations Series, 2018), 3–19.

Al-Bustani, Idlid, 'Henry and Amelia', introduced and translated (with Arabic text) by Elizabeth Holt, in Tarek El-Ariss (ed.), *The Arab Renaissance: A Bilingual Anthology of the Nahda* (New York: Modern Languages Association, Texts and Translations Series, 2018), 247–60.

Halevi, Sharon, and Fruma Zachs, '*Asma* (1873): The Early Arabic Novel as Social Compass', *Studies in the Novel* 39: 4 (Winter 2007), 416–30.

Hayek, Ghenwa, 'Experimental Female Fictions; Or, the Brief Wondrous Life of the Nahda Sensation Story', *Middle Eastern Literatures* 16: 3 (2013), 249–65.

Lindner, Christine B., 'Rahil 'Ata al-Bustani, Wife and Mother of the Nahda', in Adel Beshara (ed.), *Butrus al-Bustani: Spirit of the Age* (Melbourne: IPhoenix Publishing, 2014), 49–67.

Sheehi, Stephen Paul, *Origins of Modern Arab Identity* (Gainesville, Fl: University Presses of Florida, 2004).

Womack, Deanna Ferree, *Protestants, Gender and the Arab Renaissance in Late Ottoman Syria* (Edinburgh: Edinburgh University Press, 2019).

Zachs, Fruma, 'Feminism for Men: A Note on Butrus al-Bustani's Lecture on the Education of Women (1849)', in Adel Beshara (ed.), *Butrus al-Bustani: Spirit of the Age* (Melbourne: IPhoenix Publishing, 2014), 113–30.

Zachs, Fruma, 'Subversive Voices of Daughters of the *Nahda*: Alice al-Bustani and *Riwayat Sa'iba* (1891)', *Hawwa: Journal of Women of the Middle East and the Islamic World* 9 (2011), 332–57.

A CHRONOLOGY OF THE AL-BUSTANI FAMILY

1819 Butrus al-Bustani, Alis's father, is born in Debbieh, Lebanon.

1826 (Mar.) Rahil 'Ata [al-Bustani], Alis's mother, is born in Beirut.

*c.*1830 Butrus al-Bustani begins study at 'Ayn Waraqa Maronite College.

1834 Rahil 'Ata begins attending the school started by American Protestant missionary Sarah Smith.

1835 Rahil 'Ata joins the household of Sarah and Eli Smith.

1836 Sarah Smith dies in Cyprus.

1840 Butrus al-Bustani graduates from 'Ayn Waraqa.

*c.*1840 Butrus al-Bustani moves to Beirut.

1843 Rahil's mother tries to arrange a marriage for her; later in the year, Butrus al-Bustani and Rahil 'Ata marry.

1844 Sarah al-Bustani, the first of nine children, is born.

1846–8 Butrus al-Bustani teaches in 'Abay, at the American Protestant missionary school.

1846 Salim al-Bustani is born in 'Abay.

1847 Butrus al-Bustani and others found the Syrian Society for Acquisition of the Sciences and Arts

1848 Butrus al-Bustani, Nasif al-Yaziji, and American missionaries embark on a translation of the Bible into Arabic.
The Evangelical Church of Beirut is founded by Beirutis including al-Bustanis.

1849 Butrus al-Bustani delivers his lecture, 'Ta'lim al-nisa" (Education of Women) to the Society.
Idlid (Adelaide) al-Bustani is born.

1848–1860s Butrus al-Bustani publishes textbooks and other works.

late 1840s–1862 Butrus al-Bustani serves as official translator (dragoman) to the American Consulate in Beirut

1853 Luwiza (Louisa) al-Bustani is born.

1856 Sulayman al-Bustani (cousin; elder brother of 'Abdallah) is born in Ibkishtin.
Maryam al-Bustani is born.

1857 (Jan.) Eli Smith dies.

late 1850s The Bustanis begin to draw apart from the American missionaries in Beirut.

1858 Butrus al-Bustani and others found the Syrian Scientific Society (al-Jam'iyya al-suriyya al-'ilmiyya).

1859 Amin al-Bustani is born.
Butrus al-Bustani delivers his famous lecture on the state of Arab culture, 'Khutba fi adab al-'arab'.

1860–1 Following the outbreak of strife, Butrus al-Bustani publishes his series of broadsheets calling for unity, *Nafir suriya* (translated as *The Clarion of Syria*).

1861 Butrus al-Bustani's translation of *Robinson Crusoe* is published.

1862 Najib al-Bustani is born.
Salim al-Bustani takes over his father's post as interpreter at the American Consulate in Beirut.

1863 al-Madrasa al-wataniyya is founded in Beirut, based at the Bustani home.

1866 Sarah al-Bustani (Butrus's and Rahil's eldest child) dies in Beirut.

1867 Nasib al-Bustani is born.

1869 Butrus al-Bustani completes his dictionary, *Muhit al-muhit* (Ocean of oceans).

1870 Alis al-Bustani is born in Beirut.

al-Jinan, the first al-Bustani-edited periodical, is founded in Beirut.
Idlid al-Bustani's story 'Hinri wa-Imilya' (Henry and Amelia) is published in *al-Jinan*.

1871 Two further periodicals, *al-Janna* and *al-Junayna*, are founded in Beirut.

1876 Volume 1 of al-Bustani's encyclopaedia, *Da'irat al-ma'arif* (Compass of knowledge), appears in Beirut.

1877–87 Volumes 2–9 of the encyclopaedia are published in Beirut.

1880 Bakurat Suriya is founded by women in Beirut.

1882 Salim al-Bustani assumes editorship of *Da'irat al-ma'arif.*

1883 (May) Butrus al-Bustani dies in Beirut.

1884 Salim al-Bustani dies in Beirut.

1886 Alis becomes a member of the Beirut Evangelical Church.

1891 *Sa'iba* is published in Beirut.

1892 (Feb.) *Sa'iba* is mentioned in a reader's article in *Lisan al-hal.*
(Mar.) *Sa'iba* is praised in *Lisan al-hal* (a piece reproduced from *al-Ittihad*).

(Apr.) *Sa'iba* is reviewed favourably in *al-Muqtataf.*

1894 (Feb.) Rahil 'Ata al-Bustani dies in Beirut.
Alis and others, including her sister Luwiza and Luwiza's husband Khalil Sarkis, found the Evangelical Independent Church in Beirut.
(Apr.) Alis delivers an oration at a commemorative ceremony for her mother and Sarah Smith.
(May) Alis's oration is published in the American Missionary Press 'Bulletin'.

1897 (July) Alis al-Bustani and 'Abdallah b. Khattar al-Bustani are married in Beirut.

1898, 1900 Volumes 10–11 of the encyclopaedia are published in Cairo.

1902 Nabil al-Bustani, only child of Alice and 'Abdallah al-Bustani, is born in Dayr al-Qamar, Lebanon.

1904 Sulayman al-Bustani's celebrated translation of the *Iliad* is published.

1905 Alis, 'Abdallah, and Nabil al-Bustani move to Cairo.

1911 'Abdallah founds the Dr Abdallah Bustany Cigarette Company.

1913 Nasib al-Bustani dies in Cairo.
Sulayman al-Bustani appointed Minister in the Ottoman government.

1914 Sulayman al-Bustani resigns from government in protest over the empire's entry into the First World War.

1919 Najib al-Bustani dies in Cairo.

1923 Luwiza al-Bustani Sarkis dies in Beirut.

1925 Sulayman al-Bustani dies in New York.

1926 Alis al-Bustani dies in Cairo and is buried in the Maronite Cemetery.

1933 Idlid al-Bustani Sarkis dies.

1950 (Feb.) 'Abdallah b. Khattar al-Bustani dies in Cairo and is buried with Alis in the Maronite Cemetery.

[Author's preface, in Arabic*]

Presentation of this Volume

*Tendered to the Honoured Threshold of His Most Sublime Highness**

THIS novel, though it cannot be counted amongst works truly befitting presentation to Your Royal Presence, I presume to offer, relying on those most regal sympathies, on that succour and support that deserve and demand our utmost gratitude. Such is the pinnacle of honourable generosity, bestowed upon all of your subjects by your true and sincere kingly grace, by which you thereby adorn those subjects with your favour.

Among these grateful subjects are the community of women, who by Your Grace have been granted the light of knowledge, in this era so well-fortified by learning.* I present this work as one contribution to preserving and perpetuating what is due to this female collectivity, such rights as are due being already well-known and recognized,* and myself being a member of this group. And so, I have ventured to construct this literary piece, ordering its parts as best I could and composing it in writing. In all conditions and situations, the final word of command, and the imperial *firman*,* are the sole province of the Possessor of Grace and Charity, the Master of Valour and Power, He who commands awe and exercises strength and capability, our Sultan and guardian of our prosperity, Who does so in utter magnanimity, expecting no gratitude in return.

Your servant,
Alis Butrus al-Bustani

RIWAYAT SA'IBA

by

Al-Sayyida Alis Butrus al-Bustani

1

WHO is it at the door, Khayzuran?*

Upon my word—the matron sighed to herself—every time I make plans to go out to the shops,* I find visitors descending on me in droves! It's as if God Himself has decided to intervene, with His own plan to stay this wedding. But then, there's my sister Afifa . . . she is certainly depending on me to fit her daughter out for this union.

Khayzuran, come in here! Who is there, who has come?

Saniyya Khanim is here, my sayyida.* I have told her that you are making yourself ready to go out shopping. Here she is.

Ahh, Saniyya, greetings to you! How welcome you are—I have so longed to see you.

Pardon my coming to you in this way, my dear Fahima. I did learn that you were planning a visit to the shops and I vowed to myself that I would accompany you.

What good fortune, indeed! I have been truly uncertain over it—to whom I should turn for the advice I need. There are particular purchases I must arrange. It is your care and concern that bestow this wonderful sense of obligation—your concern that has led you here, to support me aided by your excellent taste.

I do long to be of help to you, in every way that I possibly can be! May I serve you with my very eyes and heart! Especially since this news of the marriage of your niece is abroad—it is on everyone's tongues. Yes, your sister's daughter Sa'iba is the talk of the town. But now I must remind you of your promise—and I have heard it from you more than once. You promised to let me hear this story of yours: the tale of your sister* Afifa and her daughter.

Indeed, I will tell you it all, the whole story, as we are making our way to the shops. Please excuse me for a few moments while I arrange my outdoor costume properly.* Khayzuran will bring you coffee.

And so, here we leave Saniyya alone,* sitting in the parlour, waiting for her friend Fahima. We take this opportunity to furnish our reader with a brief portrait-sketch of the two women.

The household of this Binbashi—Lieutenant Colonel Faridun Bey,* husband of Fahima Khanim—was situated near the Bosphorus,* in the sublime city of Istanbul.* Its four large chambers surrounded a broad, marble-floored reception room. The furnishings were unassuming: low banquettes and simple divans.* In niches, on recessed wooden shelves, sat attractive ceramic basins and ewers; the flowering shade plants and greenery tumbling from them had been chosen with care. The spacious chambers onto which this central atrium gave were likewise furnished with an elegant simplicity that expressed the delicate taste of those who lived here. Most especially would these rooms impress on visitors how careful, how judicious, was the administration of the lady who presided over this household. Upon inspection, one could tell immediately that she was an excellent manager. After all, she had studied—she had learned her refinement—in the schools of Istanbul.*

This lady was fair of complexion and quite tall, her figure and her limbs pleasingly harmonious and symmetrical. She had blue eyes and tawny hair, though her hair was shot through with strands of grey for she had recently passed her fortieth year. Yet Fahima's form did not betray her age. Unlike this lady, Saniyya was short of stature and rather stout, with a darker complexion although it tended to sallowness. Her opaque black eyes suggested no sense of engagement with her surroundings.

As soon as Fahima had left Saniyya on her own in the sitting room—having gone to dress for their little expedition—Khayzuran, who served this household, entered with coffee on a tray. Saniyya had time for only one sip before Fahima reappeared, swathed in her long farajiyya, a yashmak stretched across her nose and dangling over her lower face. In her hand was a leather bag of the sort that had become customary for ladies to carry on their visits to the souk. The two women sat together for a few moments as they waited for the jariya* to conclude a few household tasks so that she might accompany them.

What a perfectly lovely day it is, Saniyya! Look around yourself, see the fine prospect that Nature supplies, clothed in her springtime youth! These blossoms—their fragrances—the purity of Lady Nature's sky. How it all does stir up one's sense of poetry! Do you not see this happy swell of people? How they move about so briskly, finding something to entertain them at every turn in the brilliance of this day, eager to bask in its glow. I have no doubt that we, too, will find our proper share of joy and good fortune on this morning. Let us go on, then! And I will tell you the story of my sister and her daughter, from beginning to end. Khayzuran, ho there! Follow us—and will you shut the door tightly behind us and secure it. Here—Saniyya, at long last, listen to what I have to tell you.

Afifa—my sister Afifa—married five years after I did. The man who married her was Bahjat Bey, Defterdar* of the Governorate of Salonica.* As a Treasury official responsible for record-keeping, he was a most intelligent, honourable, and resolute man. Because of these qualities he excited the rising attention of senior men of state, and they brought him into their circles. My sister Afifa gave him two sons, but both boys passed away in their childhood. Then she gave birth to her daughter Sa'iba. But dear Afifa was badly distressed by the childbirth fever. In her ailment she was obliged to find a milk-nurse for Sa'iba. She chose a woman who had recently given birth to a girl-child but was widowed within days after the baby's birth. When my sister employed her, she took in the woman's daughter as well. That girl became a sister to Sa'iba, a constant companion.* They have been together, inseparable, ever since.

It was not long after Sa'iba's sixth birthday—continued her aunt—that her father died while on a work assignment. All he left for his family was an income of only a few months' duration.* And thus my sister Afifa, consumed and worn down by the grief she felt over her late husband, fell into a state of worry and despondency to the point of suffering grave depression. Her husband had amassed no wealth—apart from his salary—with which she could assure a livelihood. It is true that he had held several weighty administrative positions in his time. But he was a fiercely principled man, rather proud and self-denying, who refused to take even one para* above his regular salary. He spent most of what he acquired on his household, and whatever remained he gave to the poor. But the State—those who had witnessed his worthy comportment, and who knew that his family had not the means to keep itself alive—assigned a stipend to the bereaved woman and ordered the disbursement of funds sufficient to provide Sa'iba and her milk-sister Soraya with a goodly training—indeed, a considerable education in one of Istanbul's most excellent and refined schools for girls. When Afifa returned to Istanbul from Salonica following her husband's demise, a house was designated for her and to this day, that is where she lives.

As Fahima was speaking, the jariya broke in, wanting to draw her notice to a certain shop. That one surely stocks the fabrics you are looking for, said Khayzuran to her mistress.

Good, good—then lead us there, Khayzuran, said Saniyya. Let us go and see what this merchant has to offer.

Amongst all of Istanbul's shops, this establishment enjoyed particular popularity.* It was known for its fine-quality stuffs and reasonable prices, and the ladies made some purchases. As they were leaving, their eyes fell on a comely young man whose presence could scarcely be ignored. Of a light complexion and blue-eyed, he was clothed in the latest of fashions and his figure exuded an elegant perfume. His swagger told the onlooker that he was well satisfied with the dandified spectacle that his person offered.*

Do have a careful look at that young fellow! said Fahima to her companion. He has had a rather major involvement in my sister's story. I will tell you all about him when we have finished our errands.

They entered another shop, and then another, until finally they had purchased every item that they had set themselves to find.

Fahima, let's hire a boat, shall we! exclaimed Saniyya. A little outing on the Bosphorus—that's a better setting in which to hear all the rest of what you have to tell.

A fine idea! responded Fahima. And very soon, they engaged a boat and were on the water. The atmosphere was turbid,* the sky overcast with heavy but patchy scattered clouds that cast a curtain of shadow rolling across the water and darkening the surface, now and again breaking to expose shots of light. The cloud drapery deflected the sun's heavy heat and cloaked the watery expanse in a glorious mantle of shifting tones. The little rowboat sliced through the ripples, propelled by the perfectly rhythmic energy of six oars, while the two ladies observed the crowds of people on the shore. Their gazes traced the outlines of colourful palaces, houses, and gardens, each one vanishing swiftly as the boat shot smoothly by. Soon they were drawing near to one of the city's most famous boulevards. Buoyed on the sea breezes, the din assailed their ears: the screech of wheels turning, the clop-clop of hooves against the paving stones, snatches of conversation between people on the street mingling with the shouts of others who were shoving their way forward along the quay, seeking berths on a small private steam packet. As those people tried to embark, a fight seemed to be breaking out with the shipping firm's employees who were trying to stem the tide of people elbowing their way forward. The ladies' own little boat went on by, passing several other streets and jetties, and reaching the broad expanse of the Bosphorus.*

Now—tell me more of your sister's history, Fahima, begged Saniyya. Just as you promised you would! And so Fahima resumed her story.

At the age of seven—as Fahima explained to her friend—Sa'iba was enrolled in Darüşşafaka School* in the city. Soraya entered with her. They were an admirably well-matched pair in their studies, always progressing at a fine pace. They were alike in their comportment, too. Their teachers quickly discerned signs of intelligence in both girls, along with strong indication of their diligence and seriousness. Those lady teachers exerted every effort to educate the two girls until they were as refined in task and temper as could be.

Not far from Darüşşafaka sat the home of Hidayat Bey, brother of Bahjat Bey. A wealthy merchant, was Hidayat Bey. But he passed away, leaving one son, named Farid. That is the fellow we saw as we left the merchant's shop. As a boy, this Farid was cradled in luxury. He was cherished and coddled. His mother took no pains whatsoever to train or educate him—no care to shape or build his character. She was confident that the inheritance his deceased father had left to him would spare her son any need to exert himself in life.

Farid and his cousin Sa'iba were of nearly the same age, and both were clever, quick-witted, and handsome. Their families began to speak of their betrothal as a matter of course. After all, this event that appeared so inevitable would unite the two branches of the family. And so, as he grew into his young manhood, Farid still had a measure of freedom to see his cousin.* Whenever she had a school holiday, he visited her at home. As children, they had played together.

When Sa'iba and her sister Soraya were fifteen years old, they completed their studies. They had learned excellent Turkish, demonstrating skill and polish in all aspects of the language and its arts. They had become adept at embroidery and well-versed in the arts of home management. They earned very high marks in comportment and religiosity, and the two of them took many prizes. They graduated from Darüşşafaka to a chorus of congratulations and good wishes from their teachers and classmates. The school's head teacher recorded their names in the register of highest-achieving pupils, a most desirable honour, for this was a roster to be submitted humbly, in due course, to the Sublime Threshold of His Sultanic Majesty.

And Farid? *His* learning—declared Fahima Khanim to her friend—went no further than acquisition of the barest understanding of reading and writing. Infatuated as he was with tales of chivalry and romance,* he fell in with contemptible company. His band of ill-suited companions went everywhere with him, and he followed them wherever they went. And so it was that the only skills Farid acquired were those of exhibiting the trappings of manly behaviour and gamesmanship, as well as every other means of entertainment and dalliance he could find. He gave himself over entirely to his passions—his whims and fancies. He grew accustomed to having his own way in everything, no matter how outlandish his demands. No wise counsel could touch him. The words of guidance that his tender, doting mother now uttered could not tame him. As he grew older, such habitudes as he had developed only grew with him.

Farid's attachment to Sa'iba grew, too, expanding to fill his heart. But she felt no inclination towards him. Still, my sister Afifa did hold on to her longtime desire to unite the two of them in marriage as they were already bonded by kinship. She hoped that marriage would soften and refine Farid, by virtue of the values that Sa'iba could impart to him—the excellent moral character and praiseworthy principles that he must certainly witness in her.

By the time Farid turned seventeen he had already run through most of his fortune. This was mostly due to his gambling habit and the lowlife company he had been keeping as well as the hours he spent lounging in the city's pleasure palaces. His mother exhausted herself trying to win him over through her amiable and affectionate management of him. She feared most grievously for him as to the consequences of his behaviour. Earnestly did she hope that marriage would mend his ways. At this point she decided she must have a word with him. She hoped to probe his desires and understand his preferences. At once, he confessed to her that he was in love with Sa'iba. He moaned of the wrenching pain that had been his lot ever since the sanctioned practices observed between men and women had lowered a curtain that separated her from him.* He asked his mother to betroth him to Sa'iba. Would she go to Sa'iba's mother and ask for his cousin's hand? Her son's request buoyed the mother's spirits; she saw her son's desires in the mirror of her own. She had great hopes of succeeding with Sa'iba. In fact, she had no doubt of persuading the girl to accept him. She hurried to the home of my sister Afifa and there they sat together, and then were closeted with Sa'iba. They reminded her, at great length, of her cousin's many good qualities and repeatedly told her how very strongly attached he was to her.

The two women said many things, and their sweet, imploring words surely issued from their parental tenderness. But Sa'iba dumbfounded them—indeed, she silenced them with her firm responses. She refused Farid, absolutely and unequivocally. She was too young, she said, and she had no desire to marry. Sa'iba avoided saying anything that would cast doubt on Farid's status or wound his feelings. She simply remained firm about keeping herself in an unattached state.

That is—until Lutfi Bey asked to marry her. Sa'iba accepted him, having been told of his superb conduct and fine manners, his upstanding character, and his praiseworthy attributes.

By now the little boat had completed its usual circuit. The boatmen returned them to the landing across from Fahima's house. There they said their farewells and went their own ways, each to her own home.

2

THE panoramic vistas of Istanbul are well celebrated, and the beauty of its geographical location is legion, elevating it above all other cities of the world. Istanbul is unique for the bounty that Nature has bestowed upon it: the waters, the skies, the fruits and grains and all variety of growing things; and the islets and inlets, apportioned along the banks of the Bosphorus. The onlooker may contemplate—beyond these waters, and rising high above them—tier upon tier of monuments, sacred complexes, and dwellings: palaces, modest houses and large estates, set amongst lush gardens and orchards. Here is a skyline graced with cupolas and domes and minarets. The city's historic edifices hold travellers captive: comers to the city spend day after day studying their beauty. And these visitors pause to admire the abodes of knowledge here, chief amongst them the Sultanic Colleges.* Amongst these are the Imperial Military College, and the schools of medicine, engineering, naval and maritime training, artillery, industry, agriculture, commerce, and law. Hundreds of educational institutions exist here, and a vast tonnage of gold has been expended in order to build and embellish and equip them all. And then there are the printing presses, newspaper bureaus, and factories—enough to make any world capital proud. Ever since our sovereign, the Most Magnificent Sultan, Gazi Abdülhamid Khan, mounted to the exalted seat of the Ottoman Caliphate,* he has brought light to these lands—the radiance of equality and knowledge.* For these houses of knowledge and industry, he has carried forward the work that his predecessors began. He issued orders that elementary Qur'an schools, primary schools, and madrasas be established for the people throughout Ottoman territories and even in the lowliest and poorest villages.* These were the schools that prepared pupils for the higher institutions of learning in Istanbul. Boys' and girls' schools alike there are, for every creed and nationality.

We want to mention especially the military schools of Istanbul,* unique of their sort and complete in their offerings, attracting the most famous professors to their corridors, those who are most skilled in the military arts. These establishments offer instruction in all of the necessary disciplines, theoretical and practical. The Ottoman generals who have studied in these military colleges are highly practised at the arts of war and proficient in the most widely spoken Western languages—French, German, and occasionally Russian. Those among them dedicated to the naval arts most often learn English. In the Hamidian era, the time of our gracious sovereign, military service has become the profession of choice: Ottoman subjects have flocked to it, impelled by an unerringly formed desire arising from their true sense of patriotic belonging and devoted loyalty to the state. They bring to their service the fine principles instilled in them in the state's schools. To this training they join those qualities that are both instinctive to them and further polished by their upbringing: obedience, an eager longing to strive hard for the sake of their government, and—not the least—the equity and fairness they have experienced first-hand as men of the state. For such an officer is protected from unfair dismissal during his lifetime, and his family is assured of never knowing need after his death. He will advance as long as he gives faithful service and conducts himself with all due propriety and seriousness. These are but one facet of the great beneficence of His Majesty the Sultan, of his exalted good works in so many areas of endeavour that they exceed the limited capacity of human description.

Sa'iba's betrothed, Lutfi Bey, had studied at the Military College. Upon graduation he secured a good senior position as an officer in the Istanbul-based garrison.* It all unfolded in harmony with his wishes. He was the offspring of a venerable family and he owned a goodly number of houses and shops inherited from his father. Based in Istanbul, he was able to continue managing these properties in person. People knew his family of origin as honourable, and they knew his generosity too. Indeed, many individuals swarmed around him, fawning over him with grandiloquent praise. A crowd of pleasure-seekers and gamblers particularly sought to flatter him, as they coveted his wealth. Wary, he pushed them away and carefully avoided their company.

The time has come for the reader to glimpse Lutfi Bey's attributes: for he is amongst this story's most consequential and admirable figures. He was blessed with a bronze complexion and his figure was tall, well-built, and broad-shouldered. He had a lofty, wide brow and an impressively large head; a Roman nose, black eyes, dark moustaches, and a finely-etched mouth. His smile was attractive. Studying his face, one would take in qualities of steadiness, courage, sincerity, and strength of will—and also, the onlooker might surmise a well-tempered ability to conceal or suppress his emotions. The sum of his parts lent him an aura of dignity and standing, and a slight mystique: all that one could truly glean was that here dwelt patience and fortitude honed by trials of a sort. All in all, he was a figure exemplary of the finest manly qualities and an attractive, open demeanour, even if he was not generally considered truly handsome.

Lutfi Bey's residence sat adjacent to the house that Sa'iba's mother had been given. The windows of the room where he sat to work overlooked her garden. Peering through the tree branches, he could get glimpses of Sa'iba and he began to sense a growing fondness for her image. His inclinations were boosted by the words he heard from his female relatives: this girl was said to exhibit excellent comportment. She was known for her fine character and for the distinctive quality of her education. She was, in sum, a refined and polished young woman. And so, Lutfi Bey dispatched these family matrons to ask for her hand, as we alluded to in the first chapter. There followed days of parley—imparting information, seeking answers to questions, exchanging the customary usages and formalities. The betrothal contract was signed in the presence of imams and men of the religious sciences. The wedding date was set. The festivities would take place very soon thereafter.

Lutfi Bey readied a home he owned on the Bosphorus,* for his present residence was too small to accommodate all of the new furnishings he had purchased and the domestic staff he had selected. Amongst his properties, his choice had fallen on this one for its fine prospect, good construction, and handsome ornament. It was a house of two storeys surrounded by a fine walled orchard with its own pond and a garden gate giving on to a private landing. He chose the most tasteful and elegant of furniture. For Sa'iba, he had two adjacent rooms redecorated, and for himself, a room with a door leading into her apartment. For Sa'iba's mother and her sister Soraya, he fitted out three rooms across from theirs—for the mother could not endure being separated from her daughter, and they had promised each other faithfully that they would always reside together.

As for Sa'iba—she had a fair complexion and tawny hair, and limpid sky-blue eyes beneath fine lashes. Her nose had a Grecian aspect and her mouth was small and coral-like. Her throat reminded one of a gazelle's graceful outline. Her figure was elegant and stately, and just full enough. Her fingernails were the image of silver pen-nibs, and the palms of her hands were attractively plump and shone a healthy pink. Her wrists were elegantly translucent, revealing the blue veins running beneath, as though her arms had been carved from a slab of delicately coloured, veined marble. Her unpretentious taste and her contentment with the graces the Creator had bestowed upon her were evident in her simple, unadorned hairstyle: she wore her hair parted at the centre and falling loosely down her back like a cascading sash of golden ripples. Altogether, Sa'iba was the epitome of that quality of human beauty which quickens the heart and gladdens the eye. Recall the poet's lines!*

A maiden's beauty brings joy to heart and gaze:
As though on her brow cluster the Pleiades

Or these—

She fortified her countenance inside walls of light—*
worthy is that face of protective might!

And so, the appointed time arrived. With all due celebration, Sa'iba was wed to Lutfi Bey. He fêted her along with her relations, and he laid out a sumptuous feast for his friends and acquaintances.* The festivities formed the substance of many a conversation for days thereafter; the event was admired by all as having united splendour, taste, and joy. The ladies described Sa'iba's white gown strewn with pearls, her throat graced by a diamond necklace and her head encircled by a wreath of flowers fixed by pearl hairpins. In her right hand the bride held a bouquet of lemon-blossoms, and from the folds of her lovely gown peeped an entire garden of pure-white flowers. Her husband was in raptures, dazzled by her beauty as he lifted the face-veil, according to the dictates of custom. For her part, Sa'iba was overjoyed at what she saw in her new husband, for the marks of trustworthiness, gravity, and dignity were etched on his features. He wore his uniform well, a sword strapped to his waist and his Majidi medal* prominently displayed. The couple received the congratulations of a multitude.

And here our pen pauses, for it is unequal to further description of this happy moment. We make excuses for it, and we give it a well-deserved rest in anticipation of the events we shall encounter in the chapter to follow.

3

WHEN people of the East* decide to marry, they follow practices different to those of the Europeans. A European man will spend days, or months, in the company of his intended bride. The pair reveal their secrets to each other and share their sentiments on many subjects, to the point that each becomes as knowledgeable of the inclinations of the other as they are of their own. This custom is a necessity, given the rights women have obtained in Europe—which sometimes equal the rights men have—as well as the freedom women enjoy and the status they are able to insist on. Not to study his companion's character closely would expose a man to the risk of regret once he is married, for he might encounter in his wife a nature contrary to his own, a character repugnant to his taste. And also, amongst most Europeans, marriage is a bond that is indissoluble save in death.

Amongst Easterners, to the contrary, no shared sociability is permitted in advance of the wedding. At the time of life when daughters are customarily wed, they are as yet young girls whose characters have not fully matured. That is, they are married at a stage when a young female's inclinations and personality are still in formation; when she is receptive to a man's influence upon her such that her character assumes the colouring of his and she grows accustomed to the habits that he has already acquired. He is helped in this circumstance by the authority he can exercise over her—his precedence in law as much as in understanding. She learns to fear that if she behaves poorly, or rebels, he will divorce her or do her injury.* All of this conduces her to obedience: she shall be led by his hand. Thus, spending time together before marriage, as the Europeans practise, is of little necessity or utility for those of the East.

The Eastern man spends the first weeks after the wedding fully in the company of his wife. Every day he reads a new page of her nature and discovers a new side to her character. He strives to implant in her his own ways and preferences. She finds her way to him by thoroughly absorbing these aspects of his character. It is this practice that gives the honeymoon far more importance for Easterners than is true for the Europeans—and makes of it a most entertaining and pleasurable time for the married pair.

Lutfi and Sa'iba spent their honeymoon in blissful ease, sipping the nectar of joy and exchanging words of love. He was most gratified to find that she had such a sweet temper, an amiable and acquiescent nature, firm intelligence, the self-restraint of a pure soul, a refined sensibility, and a good knowledge of household management.* In turn, Sa'iba was delighted by the tenderness, the pleasant and unaffected manners, the learning and fine speech she found in her husband, as well as the straightforward, simple habits he practised in his daily life. They enjoyed long conversations on all manner of topics; the hours passed without their noticing the time. He would go off to the barracks* where he was stationed to perform his professional obligations, coming home borne on the wings of love. Sa'iba was there at the door to meet him, her voice and face eloquent with crystalline expressions that gave voice to the profound attachment she felt. They would stroll into the garden, starry-eyed, to wander together along the paths bordered in flowers and greenery. Sa'iba recounted the events of her day, not failing to include every particular, no matter how slight.

After you left the house, I tidied my room and your study.* And then I heard a loud squeal from outside—it was our neighbours' daughter. I opened the window and asked her mother if all was well. After that, I sat with my mother and Soraya, who played the oud for us and sang this song.*

Love! Submit—to your very entrails,* for passion's no easy sailing
 and Love's elect, though they be clever, will find their spirits failing
Or then, live without it, for Love's comfort is but a bane:
 it begins in wasting illness and ends when one is slain.

If it really is true—remarked Sa'iba gravely—that slaying is the end of love, then surely this can only be so because one of the lovers sacrifices their whole self for the beloved's sake.

You are undoubtedly right, replied Lutfi. The finest love is that which so perfectly permeates the soul that it becomes an indivisible part of the self. Such a sacrifice is surely made by the one of the pair who is the stronger, doing so for the weaker. It is better that the woman be the one for whom sacrifice is made. If God were to decree—shall we just say—that someone would alight right here, on this spot, from beyond that garden wall, with the intention of killing you, there is nothing I would think more perfect—more desirable to me—than that I would be the one who gives himself in sacrifice for you.

At his words, Sa'iba cried out and leant her head against his shoulder. Ya Sidi,* why do you mean to wring my heart with such thoughts? Do you not know that my life depends on yours, and your death would also be mine!

Lutfi dried her tears on his handkerchief and planted a kiss on each eyelid.

I am certain that my love for you exceeds the love that any other man feels for his wife. Whenever I am apart from you, I can only dream of you, and when we are together again, my raptures grow even stronger, as they blend with a sort of *sympathy* I feel, or what I might call a feeling of tenderness so powerful one could only think it extreme. And then—at that moment, feeling this—I am suddenly and completely filled with a consuming fear for you. I sense myself afraid for you from every source that be, but also from every thing that does not exist in this world.

And I! she exclaimed. I forget the very world itself when you are near! But—were you to be distanced from me—that might be what would kill me—what would make of me a sacrifice.

Truly, the love that Sa'iba and Lutfi shared was beyond the comprehension of ordinary intelligence, for it could not be compared to the customary love that obtains between a married pair. Nor was it surpassed by the bond between the most passionately devoted lovers imaginable. They spent their most delicious moments in the garden, strolling until they might be stopped by the sight of a soaring bird or a fluttering butterfly; or they would pause, entranced, at an opening flower, the vivid flash of an intensely colourful blossom. At the edge of the pond, a spreading willow tree shaded them.* On Lutfi's weekly days off, they liked to sit beneath the tree, poetic thoughts engulfing them in its shadow.

On this evening, as Lutfi and his wife spun together the threads of pleasant conversation, the willow branches swept them with a soft drizzle akin to the gushing tears of love, pulling them from their reverie. They saw that the sun had disappeared and the air had darkened to a gloom. They returned to the house, intoxicated by the wine of romance.

4

Reader, from listening to the conversation between Fahima and Saniyya, you have learnt that Farid was Sa'iba's cousin on her father's side, son of his late brother. But, to this point, we have kept concealed from you the particulars of that life for which he was known in Istanbul society. It is time that you become more familiarly acquainted with him. We will set ourselves to that task now.

Let us return to an earlier moment in our story: the eve before the wedding that united Lutfi and Sa'iba. Begging your leave to do so, in some embarrassment we shall accompany you into an establishment tucked away in a corner of the Istanbul neighbourhood of Beyoğlu.* There we may observe a rather spacious hall, floored in marble and furnished with row upon row of chairs arranged to face a stage. Elevated a metre or so above the floor, the stage is bedecked with various lamps, paintings, and mirrors, hanging by silken cords along the walls. To stage left is a doorway through which the actors make their entrances from a chamber behind stage. Once inside that backstage room, one finds a pale beam of natural light filtering down from a round, crystal-paned aperture in the ceiling; otherwise, this smaller room is windowless. In one corner stands a wardrobe of medium size, about two metres tall and three metres wide. Its upper shelf holds actors' carefully folded costumes, while the bottom half is covered by stacks of playing cards. At the centre of the room sits a round table covered by a length of rough green broadcloth. A lamp burns steadily there. Around the table are four bamboo chairs, awaiting the gamesters.

Acting troupes have their turns to occupy these spaces: the actors congregate on their appointed evenings to stage their plays. On other evenings, though, come the gamblers—indeed, they are here every evening of the week when actors are not present. There is a reason why they conceal themselves in this dimly-lit back room. The Ottoman Government have banned gambling in clubs and public areas;* and the authorities have begun tailing and keeping a close watch on gamblers—more intensely than ever they did before. Some dedicated gamers have sought refuge in the lodgings of simsars, these men who act as go-betweens and procurers. Others have fled inside the homes of the wealthy as they attempt to evade the eyes of officialdom. The proprietor of the theatre we have just described is one of those individuals who have managed to keep the police deceived as they throw open their doors—which give onto duplicity and flimflam—for their own customers.

Farid and his set were amongst the patrons of this establishment, gathering in the secret room at agreed-upon times. On this particular evening, it so happened that Farid and a companion were here without further company, playing cards and laying their bets. Here you are: a brief description of them both.

Farid was of rather middling height and build, a good enough specimen of a man. He was so fair of complexion and hair as to be nearly blond. He had blue eyes and a smallish mouth. He affected a rather heedless and dissolute demeanour; he would strike you as somewhat womanish in his clothing choices and the studied movements of his limbs.* His languid features conjured rather than concealed the semblance of a shifty disposition. By now, this youth had fallen fully under the control of his passions and fancies: he was openly covetous, even craven, in his constant yet dissembling artfulness. He was a terrible spendthrift. He frequented both the refined and the crude; he humoured people of honour and the coarsest of companions. He was like a chameleon, taking on a different colouring with each new set of people. When passing his time with crass and tasteless acquaintances, he spoke their language and behaved exactly as they did, appearing to be cut of the same rough cloth. Yet, when he mixed with cultured sorts,* he could be fetchingly eloquent, if only by keeping his locutionary flights tethered to certain rather simple themes. For the evidence and learning that ought to furnish such conversations, he compensated when speaking to them with a relentless hardening of his stance. He would not be persuaded of the truth of his more refined interlocutors' way of thinking, no matter how strong were the arguments and proofs they supplied. He merely played up to them with his fawning, deceptive tongue. By this means he won them over to his fine figure, his apparently mild and amiable temper, his fashionable dress, and his facility at complying with the rules of sociability and fine company. One might hear it said—by a person who knew but one of Farid's many faces—that he was surely amongst the nicest young men there ever were. A fellow truly able to capture the heart of whoever was sitting with him!

On the evening of which we speak, Farid's companion was a Greek of about forty years, quite dark-complexioned and thickset. His large head was covered in curly black hair framing a broad face, a prominent nose, and thick moustaches. His limbs were massive. This man gave an impression of cunning and slyness; surely he had a penchant for mischief.* As he strengthened his acquaintance with Farid, he began to hone the younger man's skills according to his own predilections; and he drew Farid into a life of perpetual gambling. Through crafty deception as well as outright theft, this boon companion succeeded in pilfering a large sum of money from the younger man. But then the two of them struck up an agreement to act as one, working together hand in glove on whoever might be driven—by his own miserable luck—into their gaming. The pair of them would play tricks on the unfortunate soul, luring him in with promises of profit. This would give him to fancy that the two of them were already gambling to the uppermost limits of what the most practised gamesters aspired to; and all the while, they were planting hints that this eager neophyte could learn their base wiles well enough to practise them on others. The Greek—his name was Boulos Amin*—became Farid's close advisor, his First Secretary if you will—his wily guide along the paths of other men gone astray.

But Farid was suffering from preoccupations that turned his mind away from gambling. Boulos could tell that the younger man was distracted.

I see that you are not yourself today. Have there been any serious turns in . . . ahem . . . the issue of you-know-what? Stop messing about with the cards! Loosen up—and unburden yourself. Tell me what's on your mind. You know the saying: There's no grief not followed by relief. There's always some way out.

Yes, sighed Farid. The worst you could possibly wish on me has happened. My mother's efforts came to naught. Lutfi Bey took the prize. The wedding is tomorrow.

Can you not find a way to have the wedding delayed—there must be some poison-tipped arrow up your sleeve that surely would do the business? And then, I could contrive some means to secure you your wishes, God willing.

This won't be of any use now. But I have been able to ingratiate myself with that jariya—Marjana.* Having got us on friendly terms, I confided in her. And I have persuaded her to agree to do as much as she can to win Sa'iba over to my side. She will talk to Sa'iba about me, in hopes of getting her to favour me. This jariya will come to me tonight—as soon as darkness falls and no one can make out who she is. I'll learn then what the outcome of her efforts is. My heart tells me that Marjana *will* triumph—if she is truly devoted to helping me. Because, after all, Sa'iba does have a fondness for me, there can be no doubt of that. And could anyone, in any seriousness, prefer Lutfi over me? At least, anyone who isn't himself a dull and ignorant sort? Lutfi is certainly not handsome. And he is so undistinguished . . . so droopy. He has nothing at all to say for himself. His only passions are reading and the sciences! He is as boring and lifeless as the hump of a camel.

Glancing at his watch fob, Farid stood up. Buttoning up his jacket and trying to stand tall, straightening his back and sucking in his middle, he spoke again. It's nearly time for my meeting with Marjana. I'll come back shortly—don't leave this room. I will want your counsel on what I should do.

Farid hurried out. Boulos knew that he was likely to have a long wait. He took up some playing cards. In his mind's eye he could see an opponent sitting across the table from him. He fell into playing a round with this phantom rival. Boulos was so completely under the spell of his playing cards that he could always immerse himself immediately in this whimsical game. It seemed as though he could indeed see his opponent, if only in the mirror of his own imagination. He absorbed himself wholly in attempting to play his very best—first playing his own hand and then playing that of his adversary. So engrossed was he—and he viewed it all so seriously—that moment by moment, his certainty grew. There really was another player in this room, here in front of him. He must—absolutely must!—find a way to play on him. Yes—first to entice him, and then to get his money.

And so Boulos fished out cards from various pockets, and from his sleeves, and from the depths of his waistcoat; and then he hid some of them away again. He introduced the cards he intended, with marvellously expert flicks of his hand, for he was much practised. He had all but won this hand when suddenly, looking up, he started in fright. Farid was standing in front of him. But Boulos recovered quickly and went on organizing his hand, memorizing each card as he lay it down on the table, still calculating which ones would win and which would lose out, as any sure player would do. When Farid saw him in this attitude of deep concentration he began to giggle and then to hoot with laughter, despite his troubled and gloomy state of mind.

God keep you sound and whole, Boulos—what arts are these! You couldn't even find the patience to wait these few moments for me, so I would spare you deceiving your very own self? Who can be your opposite number, I wonder! Who could make you so keen to steal from him that you would expend the lightness of hand for which you are so well known? Or—were you afraid that you might lose this beneficial practice of yours? Is that why you fancied you were playing at cards with an opponent? God preserve you—how very reassured I feel to have you as my brother and guide!

Leave your teasing. And tell me what has happened with all of this mighty effort of yours.

Ohh . . . Marjana has cut dead my hopes. The most that she could do was to advise me to be patient. She promised me that after Sa'iba has wed, she—Marjana—will do all that she can to foment such a rift between her and her husband as will force him to divorce her. And then, there would be no one else in the arena but your servant here—and Sa'iba would accept me then. Of course she would.

That sounds quite well taken. Hmm, by the sound of it, Marjana is well-practised at cunning—she's a true Devious Dalila.* I agree with her advice. And you will attain your aim if you consent to this plan.

By now, half the night had passed. They parted, agreeing to meet in the same venue two days later. Naturally, Farid was invited to Lutfi's wedding celebrations on the morrow. He could not fail to appear.

5

In the weeks following the wedding, Farid and Boulos met frequently in the theatre's back room. They plotted out what must be done to divide Sa'iba and Lutfi, sever their relationship, and thereby serve Farid's needs. For his passion was mounting so feverishly that it was beginning to deny him the enjoyment of everyday life, and it would send him into loud rages against Lutfi. Already, ever the wily trickster, Boulos had ushered Farid into the snares of his own cunning ways. Now, he was able to exert even more control over Farid—and over a great portion of his money. Farid would not do anything without first asking Boulos whether he ought, or take the tiniest step unless it fell within Boulos's shadow. Gradually, their repeated meetings, their many conversations and arguments, yielded a plan. A trap—or rather, a series of traps—to be set for Lutfi. And this would occur through the understanding that Farid had concluded with Marjana, after great effort and much expenditure. It had paid off. Now she was fully a tool in his hands, to wield at will—just as his friend, Boulos the Wicked, could play on Farid howsoever he wished to do.

This jariya had been the property of Sa'iba's father. He had purchased her as a young girl and she was raised in their household, loyal to the family.* When Sa'iba married, she selected Marjana to be her special attendant. She trusted Marjana, having seen so many years of obedience and loyal service from her. But the dinar bears its own attractions. How many a person has been corrupted by its means! How many have been seduced and have seen their fine lives collapse into ruins! This is what Farid accomplished with Marjana. He lured her with money, and she swore an oath of obedience to him. She would serve his interests and none other.

One day, coming into his office at the military barracks, amidst a stack of newspapers and correspondence, Lutfi found a letter that stood out for its red wax seal. He opened it immediately and read the contents.

Sayyidi:

I must warn you on a matter of serious concern. Your wife Sa'iba is in love with her cousin Farid.

(Signed) One Sincerely Concerned for your Honour

The colour drained from Lutfi's face. He reread the letter, trying to deduce the source. Who could this 'concerned' and 'sincere' individual be? Perhaps Farid, he muttered. But then he told himself: A lover would never divulge his own secret. Amongst my friends and acquaintance, though, no one has access to my private affairs or to the interior of my home. And Sa'iba is too pure and chaste for such a thing to be—or for me to cast her out. We have been married not even two months. She is in love with me, and she is faithful—I am certain of it! And Farid does not see her. There must be a measure of evil interference at work here. I have no doubt of it. These words are nothing more than the fabrications of some corrupt, warped soul. I will do my utmost to keep this situation under surveillance . . . But also, I will speak to Sa'iba about Farid—and I will be watching to see whether her expression changes when I do. Surely, I will unlock the mystery of these cryptic words!*

When Lutfi returned home Sa'iba was there to meet him at the door as she always did. She noticed immediately how unusually pale he looked.

What has happened, Sidi, to upset you? Or have you been suffering from aches you have hidden from me? Tell me what the matter is, I beg of you!

She seized his hand and planted a kiss on it. He put his arm around her neck and shoulders, and she encircled his waist with her arm. They strolled out to the willow tree, with its boughs draped protectively over the pond. Lutfi's preoccupied state—his silence, so unlike him—was impossible to ignore. When they had sat down she spoke again.

I have given this willow tree a name, she said. Khaymat al-hubb—the Tent of Love. Our love has taken root and grown beneath its branches, and its generous shade has sheltered us like a bower. This tree has listened to our love-talk. With every day that passes, my love for this tree—for this Tent of Love—has grown at the same pace as my fond attachment to you. I can even sense that the many hours we have spent beneath it have impressed onto its very branches and leaves a share in our life. It's part of us now, and we are part of it. This tree's protective shadow gives me so much pleasure! Just yesterday, after you had left for the barracks, I felt a tightening in my chest, as though a piece of my life was disappearing with your departure. So I came out here, out to the willow tree, and it consoled me. Because, what it has given me as I sit here are the memorable scenes of our happy times together beneath it. This tree keeps me reminded of how pure and perfect our love is.

May it ever be as you wish, sister of my soul! This willow tree is indeed a partner in our love. Ohh, that I would find in it traces of you, as you already find mine—I would find them, if I were in your place, and you were in mine.

In his wife's company Lutfi forgot the anxieties that had wracked him that day. Yet again, he found that his whole being was drawn to her; he was wholly in love, his deepest self soon mingling with hers. In her he beheld such beauty and sweet exchange as he had never experienced in his life. In their state of bliss they remained seated beneath the willow as darkness fell over them like a vast canopy. The supper hour approached. They went inside, though both were wishing that time itself would stop—that Time would permit them to prolong the hours of their felicity. Lutfi's worries—and the dejected state brought on by the warning he had received—had vanished completely by the time he entered the house with his wife.

* *

One day soon thereafter, as Lutfi Bey sat in his study engrossed in reading the day's newspapers, Marjana came in. She was gripping a sealed letter. Holding it out to him, she said, A man came to the door and put this in my hands.

He had begun trembling even before he broke the seal. In apprehension, he read it quickly. He called after the jariya and requested that she bring the messenger in to see him. She left the room and returned moments later to say that he had gone.

Go! Try to catch up with him. If you go quickly, you probably can fetch him.

He stood up and paced around his study, and then peered through the windows, the letter still clutched in his hand.

Sa'iba leads Farid to the willow tree after her husband has left for the barracks. She prefers the early afternoon hours, since her mother and sister are sleeping then.

Sa'iba, he reflected, had told him that when she was feeling desolate, with a tightness catching in her chest, often she would go out to the willow tree seeking its shade as solace. . . . Buried in his thoughts, Lutfi did not notice the jariya's reappearance. She tried to make her presence known with a soft word but she had to make several attempts before he became aware that she was there. Finally, she got him to understand that she had hurried after the messenger but had not been able to overtake him. Lutfi instructed her to inform her mistress that he was leaving the house on important business. She should have his midday meal sent to him at the barracks.

Throughout the remainder of that day Lutfi was upset and confused. He could think only of what he must do to uncover the concealed source of this furtive, covert campaign. His work obligations completed, he hired a small boat to take him home. He mounted the steps from the landing and nearly ran to the garden gate. He yanked it open. There he saw Sa'iba, sitting under the willow tree, reading. Tears flowed down her face. He went over to her and asked what it was that had made her cry.

It's this story!—the tale of Geneviève with her husband.* How it was that those wicked, despicable people steeped in lies ruined everything between them and made their lives a misery. Those immoral liars nearly destroyed this poor unlucky woman—and would have done, if God had not shown His grace to her after she had already endured the sorts of torments that only martyrs suffer.

Her words touched Lutfi deeply. His heart thudded as he began to fear that he, himself, might be turning into the likes of Geneviève's husband; that he was becoming a mere dumb implement in the hands of a corrupt, nefarious, no-good schemer. He sat down beside Sa'iba and tried to comfort her, employing every means he could summon to draw her away from the afflictions of Geneviève. The couple went into the house to have their evening meal. But Lutfi remained imprisoned in his worries over the latest letter he had been sent. He was as confused as ever about what he ought to do. He seized the first chance he could to mention Farid's name, and he talked at some length about Sa'iba's cousin.

Before this day, whenever Farid's name came up in conversation Sa'iba found her face reddening, uncertain of how to react or respond. She did not want to speak about him: after all, he was her own cousin. But this time she could not remain silent. Lutfi, so intelligent and adroit at these manners of speech, directed the conversation smartly to the topic of how attached one always is to one's relatives. Indeed, how fortunate and happy one is to be blessed with an abundance of family members! For they are one's support in times of need, a resource in situations of hardship. He so wished, he said—if only the dictates of society and the faith allowed it—that she could be freely in Farid's company. He was her cousin, and he might as well be her brother, and he had such fine taste, and he was such good company and so fine-looking, and with an excellent mind, too—why, such qualities would amply compensate for any defects there might be—that is, indeed, if any such flaws existed in him!

Sa'iba bowed her head. After a moment she spoke. Of course, she loved Farid, as he was her cousin. And she saw nothing in him so flawed as to keep people from confidently accepting his company, except perhaps his spendthrift habits and his frivolity, his sometimes thoughtless ways with people. However—she said—a woman's interactions with even her male relations must be restricted and regulated, following the Sunna of the Prophet. Anyone who stepped over these boundaries was straying from the Right Path.*

Although Sa'iba appeared somewhat flustered and embarrassed as she said her piece, this was not out of the ordinary when speaking about Farid. Lutfi saw nothing in her response to raise any suspicions. Indeed, he felt a sense of relief, as though a heavy burden had just been lifted from his heart—one that had all but paralysed him. He thanked God for bestowing on him the gravity and discernment to study all matters carefully; to not be led astray by whims or terrible fancies; to remain impervious to the deceptions of those wayward souls in the world who seek to ruin the lives of others.

Sa'iba spoke up again, to complain of how melancholy she often felt. There are days, she said, when I feel utterly dejected—my heart so constricted I can't breathe—but there's no reason I know of for it. I feel as though God's hand is pressing on me and will crush me. I see a great affliction threatening my very existence—the world goes dark in my eyes. And then I long to be far away from this house. To go away with you, somewhere other than here, somewhere remote and isolated from the world where we can simply live together, happy and content with the blessings God has granted us. Last night, I had a dream in which I saw a strange phantom floating in a vast green garden of flowing rivers and ornamental trees where birds were chirping in the branches. This spirit-figure began calling me into the garden, promising me all manner of happiness and repose. The scene was so vivid that I sensed a force pulling me to it and I was powerless to resist. And then . . . you were there, and it seemed that you wished to prevent me from going, or from being taken away. You took me in your arms and you made me swear not to leave you. And so I kissed you on the mouth—a kiss that left me weak—and then I slept long and deeply. I slumbered in a place of peace I had not known before. This dream! I tried to explain it to myself as simply the aftermath of a lingering stomach upset, or of nerves, but that only caused me more confusion—as though there were some secret eating at me, but one that is too deeply concealed for me to know what it was.

All the while she spoke, Sa'iba stood facing her husband, She wore a white silken gown through which the outlines of her shoulders and collarbone were visible as they converged on her throat. The gown's sleeves were wide and ripply as if she were wearing a Bedouin robe. Her golden hair tumbled down her neck and back, tousled by the occasional light toss of her head. The lamp hanging from the ceiling poured streams of light over her. Lutfi could not suppress an impassioned response to this vision.

What appeared to you yesterday—where is all of that, compared to what I see now! That was nothing but a passing illusion. *This* is real. In your beauty, and with your sensible temperament,* can you be anything other than an angel beneath a halo of dawning light? Nothing will happen unless you wish it that way. Do not feel anxious over any of it. Tomorrow, I will ask those in charge to send me to Salonica Governorate. There we can live in the countryside, and the salubrious air will put to rest these dark thoughts you have had.

6

LET us return now to the tucked-away theatre, where we will find Farid and his friend Boulos seated in their usual places in the dressing room and reviewing the events of recent days. Sallow-faced Farid's eyelids droop. His hands grip his knees and his head swivels this way and that, as now he stares blankly into a corner of the room, and now he shifts to gaze fiercely at Boulos.

In his friend's face Farid was attempting to read something of the direction of his thoughts. From Boulos he anticipated a final judgement on his passion: would it be a sentence of despair unto death, or a ruling that said hope would live on?

Boulos, meanwhile, was toying with his deck of cards, lining the cards up in neat rows on the table and then shuffling them all together only to distribute them once again in pairs or singly. But his constantly darting eyes and flitting hands seemed to announce that his mind was occupied with something other than his cards. For some moments this scene did not change. Then, hearing carriages passing by in the street and the voices of people outside, Farid looked at his watch.

It's five o'clock in the morning, he said. We've been sitting here for seven hours waiting for that accursed woman. It seems that she is not coming. I am going to sleep for an hour. Don't wake me up—not for anything. Unless she comes.

He went over to a corner of the room and sat down heavily, reclining against a large cushion. Boulos lit a cigarette. When his friend's napping went on longer than Boulos liked, he fell back on his usual pastime, cutting the pack of cards, playing his hand, and then playing that of his pretend opponent.

Eventually—by now, it was nine o'clock European time*—muted footsteps could be heard outside the door. Boulos heard the theatre owner's voice, too.

They're inside. Do you want to go in?

Boulos opened the door. As Marjana entered Farid abruptly woke up. He lost no time in addressing her.

Your absence has kept us waiting a long time. Have you had any success?

Yesterday I put the letter into Sidi Lutfi Bey's hand, just before he went off to the barracks. I could see that he was very upset after reading it. When he came home it was by a different route than he usually takes. He came in through the garden gate, where he saw my mistress sitting beneath the willow, reading the story of Geneviève and crying. He sat with her for a short while. After they finished their supper I heard them talking, as if everything was normal. But I could see in my master's eyes—and all over his face, really—signs of distress that he was trying to conceal. I think this ruse of ours will succeed. I think that my master Farid will obtain his desires if he can but be patient. I will vouchsafe the return of my mistress's heart to him—for she has complete confidence in everything I say and do.

Farid was about to speak but before he could do so Boulos clapped his hand over Farid's open mouth. Iblis! he exclaimed. The Devil had just inspired him with a new idea! It was a trick that he was certain would be victorious—if only Farid and Marjana complied with his instructions to the letter. He turned to Marjana.

Does your master have his own private carriage?

No. But after the wedding he bought a chaise. It's got just two wheels and one seat and it is pulled by a single horse. Sometimes he drives it and sometimes my mistress does. She is very skilled at it. More than once I have heard my master tease her, saying that with her carriage-driving skills she could challenge the best coachmen in the business.

Excellent! You know the way to the forest on the northern edge of the city, don't you?

Yes. Several times I have gone there with my mistress.

Also very good. This afternoon, at three o'clock ifranji time,* go in to your mistress in a state of fright and tell her—in that cunning, persuasive manner that I know you have—tell her there is a soldier at the door and he was ordered to the house by Lutfi Bey, to inform her that he fell from his horse while riding in the forest. Say that he has been badly wounded. A head fracture. He is waiting for her in the hunters' lodge and she must come as quickly as she can. Do your utmost to convince her that she must respond to her husband's command immediately! She must go—she can drive the chaise and you shall go with her. The lodge is one hundred metres from the road: you stay with the carriage and send her on her own to the lodge. Do you understand what I am telling you to do?

And more! exclaimed Marjana. I know that when my mistress arrives at the lodge, she will find Farid waiting for her, and thus the snare is fully— . . . But what I do not see is how, even with all of your crafty schemes, you will figure out how to ensure that Lutfi Bey learns everything, and in enough detail that he will throw off his wife.

I have told you all you need to know. Take this little bag—five lira—and follow my orders, without any more chatter.

Done, said Marjana. Hah—this is what a real man is made of! I have no doubt that if Mr Farid had your knowledge, and your kind of head, his efforts would not have been so useless in the first place, or thwarted from start to finish.

Marjana hurried out. Boulos coached Farid on his role in this elaborate trick that he had devised and then they parted, promising each other to meet late in the afternoon at an agreed-upon spot.

7

Farid arrived at the hunter's lodge which sat at the edge of the forest promptly at three o'clock in the afternoon. Hunters were in the habit of gathering there in the early afternoon hours to sleep through the worst heat of the day. The lodge's ground floor comprised a large hall; above were two smaller rooms encircled by a rooftop terrace that overlooked the forest to the front and, to the rear, extended over a rocky basin through which threaded a narrow stream. The establishment's proprietor had retired for an afternoon rest. Roused by the sound of hooves, he hurried outside in time to see Farid dismount. He took the reins, led the horse to a ring fixed in the wall, and fastened the reins there. He scurried back to Farid and ushered him inside and up a flight of stairs to the upper storey.

What poor luck! fumed Farid to this man. I have still got a letter in my pocket that ought to have been posted. Here, quick now, take it to the municipal building. And here is a riyal—buy us some sweets and a bit of fruit, and hurry back as fast as you can because within the hour a group of friends are coming to meet me here.

The man hurried off to attend to Farid's errands, rejoicing in the appearance of this visitor of evident good breeding. Such generosity, such liberal spending! Upstairs, Farid sat down at the window overlooking the forest, fixing his eyes on a cluster of trees that marked the turn from the main road onto the lane leading directly to the lodge. His nerves were in a highly agitated state. He glanced at his watch repeatedly; the minutes were passing so slowly. Finally, he caught sight of an indistinct figure in the distance, walking through the little grove of trees. He suspected that it was Sa'iba. His heart began to beat wildly. He felt himself paralysed, uncertain of whether he should go and meet her in the forest or whether he ought to wait here and begin their encounter inside the lodge. He was so overcome by the tremblings of love and the palpitations of longing that his brain was addled; he was certain he was losing his mind. He stared again at his watch and saw that it was already half past three. He did not know what to do. He went over to a mirror on the wall and studied his likeness with fierce concentration. Yes, he approved of what he saw. A smile spread over his face. He examined his dress and smoothed out some creases, adjusting a fold here and another there, perfecting the drape of his costume over his body. He went back to the window. He heard the sound of a carriage and was certain it was Sa'iba's. He was readying himself to go out and meet it but just in time, he recalled that Boulos had told him to wait for her inside the lodge. Only when she was already there—so he had been instructed—would he reveal his presence to her. Still, Farid had not quite resolved himself to what he should do when he did catch sight of Sa'iba's form there in the trees, evidently trying to hurry but hampered by her long black farajiyya. Her lovely face was masked by a yashmak. As she approached the lodge, he came out to meet her, his gait typically declaring a cocksure arrogance. She was startled to see him. So taken aback, in fact, that she felt her legs give way at the sight of him. But she rallied. How was Lutfi Bey, she asked him, and had the physician been to see him?

Lutfi? Who do you mean, who is it who has seen Lutfi?—beloved of my heart! Come upstairs and calm your fears.

It is no use hiding the truth from me. I am prepared for the worst news. Tell me everything and take me to him at once.

Leading the way, Farid mounted the stairs. She was close behind. He closed and locked the door to the forest-side rooftop terrace behind her. He paused to drop the key into his pocket, wanting to keep it secure and well hidden away. She went ahead of him, entering each room in turn. But she found no trace of Lutfi. Her confusion mounted and her face went paler. She felt as though the floor was trembling and about to give way beneath her. She retraced her steps, going over to where Farid stood, still occupied with the business of safely stowing away the key. She was immediately suspicious. She knew well to be apprehensive of his devious ways. She was shaking but her voice was firm and strong.

If Lutfi is not here now, then where is he?

Oh, the Lutfi story was only a ploy to get you here. Calm down, you can feel at ease!—and do be gentle with your cousin, who loves you to distraction, and who would sacrifice his very soul for you. For—as you can see here—love has consumed him. Love has weakened him terribly, so much so that it has begun barring him from the joy of being alive.

Instantly Sa'iba understood what had happened. She saw her cousin's treachery as plainly as could be. She was aware, too, of how awkward and even dangerous this situation was for her. If Lutfi were to learn that she had left the house and had met Farid in a place where there was no one else to be seen—and worse, a spot remote from the city—the consequences would be terrible. He would sooner suffer a wound to his body than allow the prospect of a wound to his honour. And he might well not believe her if she told him honestly what had transpired. After all, had she not seen him, only two days previously, in a very odd state? Seen his mood swinging wildly, acting unlike himself, and uttering peculiar words? Her resoluteness flagged in the face of such thoughts and images. She sat down. Farid came very close to her, intent on kissing the back of her hand. Suddenly aware once again of her surroundings, abruptly she came out of her musings and pushed his hand away. Though her aversion was obvious he tried again to approach her. She moved away, stepping back until she was perched at the very edge of the rooftop terrace where it faced the stony depression. Farid stood still. He warned her of the danger of falling. She stared at him, her gaze mingling scorn with fear.

You—you treacherous man! Do you think I would sell my honour just to save my life? Stay where you are or I will throw myself off this rooftop. Unlock that door, open it so that I can go home. That is, if you have a shred of honour and manliness left in you.

Rest easy . . . Have no fears for yourself! I am nothing more than your slave, your captive. Only promise me that you will allow me your love if Lutfi leaves you.

In Farid's features Sa'iba could see the marks of a suffering man. She understood that it would not be wise to push him to the point of utter despair, lest he harm her. She knew his character: his rashness and his propensity for violence. And so she merely responded that she would not promise anything at all at the present moment. That he was her cousin; that he was like a brother and he must be her support in times of hardship. As she spoke they heard two gunshots at some distance away from the lodge.

I will suffice for now with this much. With what you have said, with this one promise of yours—until God opens the way to an opportunity eagerly awaited.

The shots were a message from Boulos. He had concealed himself near the lodge. The sound told Farid that every aspect of the scheme had gone as planned, and now he was to release Sa'iba and allow her to go home. Farid unlocked the door and opened it for her. Sa'iba went through, hardly believing that she had truly escaped this trap.

Farid closed the door behind him as he followed her out. He went to untie his horse. He found the lodge's proprietor waiting there, his arms full of fruit and sweets. He gave the man another riyal for his troubles, mounted his horse, and caught up with Sa'iba's carriage, already on its way.

As usual, Lutfi had left the house that day to go to his work at the barracks. He had been much affected by Sa'iba's words about her desire to leave Istanbul. He had taken a decision to request a transfer to one of the Empire's European vilayets. As he was thinking about how to put his request, he received an order from the military administration* to proceed at once to the city of Salonica. He would assume supervision of a provincial police force.* Without even asking, his wishes had been met! He was so pleased that he penned a hurried note to his wife at once, wanting to give her this fine piece of news. Surely, it would reassure her and calm her anxieties. The two of them would be vacating this city only two days hence. He went out to the shops immediately, wanting to make all necessary preparations for the journey. He bought some basic necessities and made the requisite arrangements. Returning to the barracks, he found several letters waiting for him. Most bore Istanbul addresses and he read them quickly. They were of such little importance that he tossed them into the bin. Except for one, which left him shivering and wiping his brow—no sooner had he perused its brief contents.

At four o'clock in the afternoon, Sa'iba will meet Farid at the hunting lodge.

As he read this sentence Lutfi felt himself exhausted, his forces depleted. His entire body broke out in a cold sweat and he took several gasping breaths. Looking at his watch, he saw that the time was already nearly four o'clock. He catapulted from his seat as if dislodged by a shock and went for his horse. Saddling it quickly, he rode towards the forest. He made his way through the trees, remaining hidden from sight whilst maintaining a path that permitted him to see everything around him. He did not have to wait long. Somewhere behind him he heard two gunshots. It was not five minutes before he saw Sa'iba and the jariya in the chaise. And then he saw Farid on horseback, close behind them. His blood seemed to freeze in his veins at the horror of what he was witnessing. He felt himself sink into utter despair. He could scarcely believe his eyes—his trust in Sa'iba had been so strong. But alas, now his own eyes had banished all doubt.

Although he was a man of great self-control, constitutionally discreet and not prone to quick reaction, here in the forest he felt as though the membranes of his heart had split apart. He made up his mind to go home immediately—and to leave Sa'iba behind in Istanbul when he went to his new assignment.

As Lutfi sat on his horse amidst the trees, in this terrible state of mind and body, he saw a hunter coming along the way. The man had a greyish beard, a swarthy complexion, and was short of stature but with a noticeably large head. A rifle swung from his shoulder and two dogs trotted ahead of him. He sang out a greeting to Lutfi, who started, as if he had been dozing only to be suddenly awakened by an unexpected presence. With some difficulty, Lutfi managed to return the greeting. The hunter appeared insensible to the scene before him, completely unobservant. It was clear that he had not taken in Lutfi's plainly evident state of affright.

Do you know anything about the lady who passed by just now in that chaise? he asked Lutfi. What a pretty one! Hearty congratulations to the young man accompanying her. As I went by the lodge a few minutes ago, I did see her chatting away freely with a young fellow.

Lutfi said nothing. He set his horse towards home, spurring it into a gallop.

8

WHEN she was finally able to escape Farid's clutches, Sa'iba hurried directly to her chaise. There, Marjana asked immediately after her master Lutfi Bey. Sa'iba, intent on setting off as quickly as possible, did not answer. When Marjana repeated her query, Sa'iba replied. I did not see your master Lutfi. The news of his fall was no more than a falsehood concocted by Farid. He hopes to make Lutfi despise me.

She was interrupted by Marjana. Oh, look—there he is, my master, hiding in the forest. He is watching us.

Sa'iba turned to look but she did not see him. Just then Farid, on horseback, reached them. Sa'iba slapped the reins against the horse's flanks to urge it on, and it broke into a fast gallop. With Farid in pursuit, they reached the streets of the city whereupon he and his horse disappeared into a side street.

Sa'iba could not stop her head from swirling sickeningly, overwhelmed as she felt by the day's events. She was in a state of nervous collapse, her body quaking as her mind relived every moment of this terrible treachery. She could not see any path open before her that would free her of the responsibility and the censure that her husband would surely impose. The carriage came to a stop in front of the house and she hurried directly to her room. Inside and alone, the emotion uppermost in her heart was grief. She cried and cried hot tears, the watery echo of a heart shattered by sadness and despair.

On that morning Sa'iba's mother and Soraya had gone to the public baths, invited by her Aunt Fahima. When she arrived at home they had not yet returned. There was no one here to console her, no one to share her terrible perturbations. She all but collapsed into a stupor. But then she heard, or she sensed, Lutfi going into his room. She washed her face and readied herself to go in to him. She would relate all that had happened; she would not miss out any detail or conceal anything. Her heart was so pure and her love for him was so vast that—even now, and in this dreadful state—she was confident that he would believe her, that he would not attempt to refute this terrible situation that Fate—not her—had visited upon him. When she pushed his door open, she found him standing at the very centre of the room. His colour had changed since she had last seen him. His demeanour, his very form, looked shrunken, as though this hour alone had added years to his age. At the sight of her he started, and passed his right hand over his eyes as though he were trying to ascertain the reality of what he saw.

Naturally Sa'iba was not accustomed to seeing him in such a condition. She was terrified; his rigid form and his unremitting silence particularly frightened her. She clutched at the bedpost to keep herself from falling as she tried to pull herself together. She began to recount all that had happened: how Marjana had given her the news that her master had fallen from his horse and had been wounded badly; that he had despatched a soldier to summon her; and on through all that had taken place with Farid. Lutfi heard her out, all the while remaining as still and as cold as a statue. He did smile, but it was a sad and wary smile. At this, Sa'iba broke into tears so bitter that they stung her eyes. She made to kiss his hand but he jerked it away from her. She knelt before him.

Sidi, she said, I know what a serious matter this is—what I was led to by what I thought was your command. I know how firm, how immovable, is your sense of honour; and how terrible it would be to see it injured. It is this that has all but landed me in utter despair. The *appearance* of all that has happened grieves me, and I know that it compromises me—yet my love for you, and Farid's treachery toward me, disguised as a trick to convince me that your life was in danger, surely must intercede for me and touch your sympathies.

Her voice was steady and she showed no signs of uncertainty. As always, her demeanour radiated purity and impeccable goodness. Lutfi did not fail to notice any of this. He softened towards her.

Nothing is hidden but that it comes to light. If you are indeed telling the truth, then no one will adhere more closely to you than myself.

But as soon as Lutfi had uttered these words he strode into his study and shut the door behind him. He spent the remainder of the day there. In the evening he left the house and returned only to go to sleep. That entire night he lay awake. Had not the hunter told him of seeing a youth and a young woman together, speaking familiarly, at the lodge? Had he not received two warnings before this most recent one? Had not Sa'iba herself told him of her hours of misery, when she would go to sit beneath the willow, seeking solace in its shade? Had he not seen how disturbed and discomfited she was; how she had blushed when he mentioned Farid's name? Were these not all testament to a love between the two of them? Yet, when she had told him of today's incident, hadn't he read the signs of sincerity in her face? And in any case, if she had been in love with Farid, then surely she would have married him when he requested her hand!

These thoughts and others tugged at him, pursuing him without pity. They left him torn between scepticism and persuasion, in the suspicions about his wife that had invaded him. He had no appetite for examining her more closely: he dreaded the possibility that doing so might only confirm her terrible sin. Sa'iba, for her part, grew ill as a result of the events of that day. Lutfi did not see her. He completed his preparations for transferring to his new appointment. Early the next morning he went to the barracks to say goodbye to the men with whom he worked. He was in a state of great anxiety and torment. Had Sa'iba been conscious of the extent of his pain, she would have been all sympathy. He was a man in love; he was not to blame for his terrible despair, just as she was not to be frowned upon for hers. Right or wrong! Both members of this pair were correct in their reactions; afflicted sorely by their predicament, both also had missed the mark.*

When Lutfi left the room, leaving her alone, Sa'iba felt her heart split in two. She saw herself facing the utmost misery and abasement. She kept to her room, weeping and moaning, distraught over her misfortune, until she became feverish. When her sister Soraya came home and went in to see her, she was astonished at the sight that met her. She tried to hold Sa'iba in her embrace, kissing her and begging her to tell her what had happened. Sa'iba—by now slightly calmer than she had been at first—related the sad sequence of events. Her quiet recital reassured Soraya somewhat. But Sa'iba's stoic demeanour forsook her as she came to describing the encounter with Lutfi and how he had shown nothing but contempt for her distress. How he had not believed her even though she had told him the truth, fully, having never, ever in her life told a lie. The doubts about her that he clearly harboured had shattered her soul. Did he not know her as his faithful, loyal, and truthful wife? Soraya tried her best to comfort and reassure Sa'iba. Gently, she wiped away her sister's tears and helped her to go to bed. But Soraya was exceedingly uneasy about the fever and she dispatched someone immediately to fetch the doctor. She returned to Sa'iba's bedside, doing her best to hide her fears.

My dear, she said to Sa'iba, to all appearances you do look guilty. It is no wonder that Lutfi would feel suspicious despite his great confidence in you and the strength of his love. The truth will all be revealed to him in a day or so, or in a few days perhaps, and your innocence and purity will be upheld. He will come back to you, apologizing as would any honourable man. So, relax yourself and try not to worry over it. And do try to keep all of this from your mother, for I know that she would be very troubled indeed if she were to see such despair in you.

Hearing her sister's words, Sa'iba exerted herself to stay strong, to maintain her fortitude, to be patient. She submitted herself to God's will.

Only a few moments later her mother came into the room. She could see traces of tears on Sa'iba's face and she asked anxiously what was wrong.

It's only the effects of the fever, said Sa'iba. I've had the chills.

The physician saw no cause for alarm. He had prescribed some relaxants along with bedrest. Sa'iba must remain in bed for several days, he said. That night she fell asleep with Soraya keeping watch at her side. In the morning the doctor returned and was pleased by the progress he saw. He ordered them to continue the sedatives and he prescribed a small dose of quinine. As the day went on, Sa'iba improved and the fever dwindled. Whenever she asked about Lutfi, Soraya told her that he was at work and would come home that evening as usual. But when Soraya had left the room to prepare some light food for Sa'iba, Marjana slipped in, bearing a piece of paper that she shoved into Sa'iba's hand. Reading it, the young woman went dizzy and fainted. At that moment Soraya was coming back into her sister's bedroom. Seeing Sa'iba's newly alarming state, she got her to sniff some reviving spirits. When Sa'iba came to, she informed Soraya that Lutfi had travelled to Salonica on important business. She gave her sister the note that Marjana had passed to her. Soraya tried to elicit some sort of meaning from it. Perhaps there was a change of plan?—an order from his superiors, that had obliged him suddenly to travel alone? But he had been so determined that the two of them would go together. Sa'iba was not persuaded by any of the possible reasons for his solitary departure, and the news of it aggravated her confusion and unease, indeed her distress. Soraya, for her part, wore herself out trying to distract her sister and to somehow cheer her spirits.

9

WHEN Farid turned off the main thoroughfare—having followed Sa'iba's chaise that far—he hurried on to the theatre. His face was glowing. He planned to wait there for Boulos to appear, ready to appraise him of every detail of the meeting between himself and Sa'iba. And he wanted to hear every particular of this manoeuvre that Boulos had kept secret. His partner did not keep him waiting for very long. Boulos was still wearing his hunter's-costume disguise.

It was almost sunset. They entered the dressing room together amidst mutual congratulations on the success of their stratagem. Farid repeated the words Sa'iba had said to him when he had cornered her on the roof terrace: that she had promised him a good outcome! Even if, first, she had berated him for ensnaring her in this trap. But upon hearing Farid's happy onrush of words, Boulos rebuked him soundly for his heedlessness. He had been wrong, said Boulos, to admit to this underhanded operation of theirs. It would have been wiser to leave her believing that it was mere happenstance bringing them together there. Indeed, Boulos went on, this feather-brained performance could have thwarted the entire plan! Farid apologized meekly. He couldn't help it! he protested. To be in such close proximity to her had set his heart on fire. The solitary meeting had augmented his desire beyond even what his feelings had been before he saw her there, and his good sense had deserted him. Boulos relented and told him that he had written to Lutfi to inform him of Sa'iba's determination to meet Farid in the hunting lodge. And then, he recounted how he had disguised himself and hidden at the edge of the forest waiting for Lutfi to arrive.

Lutfi came on horseback, Boulos said. He concealed himself amongst the thickets. That is when I fired the two gunshots to announce that it all had gone according to plan, and to sound the all-clear. He saw you, on your horse, following the chaise. As soon as you were all out of sight, I put myself in his way. At first he did not pay any attention to me, maybe he didn't even notice me—that is how upset he was. When I called out to him, he did answer. I told him I had seen that woman who had just gone by in the chaise. I saw her talking in very familiar terms with a handsome young man at the lodge, I said. When he heard this, his face darkened—I could see the blood rushing into it. He stared at me and the hard gleam in his eyes scared me—as if his brain had erupted and caught fire and sent flames all the way to his eyeballs. As I was backing away, he galloped off. Though his expression frightened me, I was wonderstruck at how calm he remained, how cool he seemed in the face of this terrible blow he had just received. Even in a state of extreme distress he appears to be a man who is above such things.

Do you think he will divorce her?

There are three choices that anyone in this dilemma could make, replied Boutrus. Divorce her—but this is unlikely if he is not certain of her guilt. Abandon her—that is more of a possibility. Or, discover the plot. That could happen, given your negligence, the way you have advertised our secrets! This would mean that all of our efforts will have turned out to be in vain. But now, we will simply have to wait until we can learn what else has happened—from Marjana herself.

Farid sighed. Just suppose the whole con does collapse. Don't you have another trick in your brain? A completely new scheme that would mean success? I think I will die if I can't collar Sa'iba.

All matters are ransom to their timing. The lion's den is never empty of bones. But I need a certain sum of money. I am just about penniless and everything costs dearly these days.

It's yours—here, a small sum. But you'll see enough of it from me to keep you happy.

A small sum—yes, it is, if not followed by more of the same! I think you will know by tomorrow what has happened between Lutfi and Sa'iba, as surely today's events will determine that. Go on now, with God's blessings, and mind you do not wag your tongue—it is certain to bring ill outcomes.

Right—I will follow your instructions. Until tomorrow then. We will meet here tomorrow, or the day after, to agree on what we must do next.

10

Lutfi took a boat to Salonica.* He remained in that city long enough to make his arrangements for travelling overland to his new posting, a town situated in the interior of the province.* Leaving Salonica, he had a small following of men with him. After a few hours in the saddle they had traversed several parasangs.* They now found themselves in a verdant expanse of well-shaded groves and fast-running streams.* They would set up their tents here, Lutfi ordered. He set off alone to wander through these coppices, breathing in the cool, refreshing breezes of the late afternoon. The sun was close to setting and the ground had attired itself in a golden wrap of fallen leaves. The air was sweet and revivifying; its gentle gusts pushed at the tree branches, shaking off whatever leaves the lingering autumn had allowed to stay in place. These garden surroundings ignited memories, as if Autumn had let loose its fiery arrows on all of Nature, drawing blood as Nature itself looked on and wept. Indeed, the melancholy scene before him deepened Lutfi's anguish; and he felt as though the very atmosphere were squeezing the breath from his body. He wandered along in his agitated state, murmuring to himself, waving his hands, and then, in a fit of panic, wheeling around abruptly to stare at what lay behind him. As the sun disappeared, it left rays of red to linger, and then paler rays of orange followed by yellow, melting finally into the dark blue horizon. The rays of light vanished and the battalions of darkness attacked. Lutfi walked on, encased in his pain and the visions he could not banish from his head. Finally, he stopped in utter confusion: for he sensed the presence of a hidden, mysterious power, driving him toward a knot of trees in the midst of which he could see a small pool of water. It was surrounded by a carpet of green marked by patches of flattened grass where something had fallen or lain. Lutfi heard a faint sound, as though a body had moved through these dense trees and had caused them to move; as if that body were still making its way in here, causing the branches to sway and shake. He plunged forward into the dark recesses, oblivious to the thorns which tore at him and left shallow gashes in his skin.

He had only to go a few steps when he saw an indistinct figure crouched there and heard the sounds of crying. Moans rose into the air. The figure's dress and features seemed to resemble Sa'iba's form—here in this forest, only a few steps away from him! He must be losing his mind. He hurried forward, his heart pounding and his whole body trembling. Like a heaving sea, his head swirled and throbbed with images and thoughts. Only inches separated them now. He felt Sa'iba's hand clutching at his arm. He heard her, whispering into his ear. *Malefactor! Tyrant!* He felt himself sinking, dropping into a faint . . .

When Lutfi awoke, it was a few seconds before he realized that one of his men was bent over him, his arm encircling Lutfi as he tried to get him to breathe into a bottle of spirits to bring him back to life. His thoughts were muddled but he was aware enough of his situation to feel uneasy. Could this man have discovered something of his plight? He got to his feet and directed the man to lead him to the encampment. He managed to avoid showing any signs of surprise or disquiet; and he did not say a word more.

The next morning, Lutfi and his little party resumed their journey at a fierce pace. In a single hour, they covered a distance that normally would have taken several hours. As on the day before, Lutfi was absorbed in thought and sensed himself deeply apprehensive. On the tablet of his mind he reviewed it all: his love for Sa'iba, her many attractions, her praiseworthy qualities. He tried to exonerate her of the suspicions his conscience had relentlessly flung at her. But every time his affections prevailed, overcoming his anxieties and putting paid to his doubts about her behaviour, suddenly there would come into his mind the image of her face bearing an expression of embarrassment; or his bewilderment as she went by in the chaise with Farid close behind her. He could not escape what her obvious discomfort and the dejected expression on her face seemed to say; nor could he forget other details all of which seemed to point to her guilt. And so he would revert to his earlier state of mind, wallowing in his doubts, and would begin to believe once again that every gesture and every word of hers was most certainly a just witness to her sinful behaviour and errant ways.

Caravans passed them by; they traversed lovely brooks and breathtaking vistas and arid stretches, but Lutfi saw none of it, immersed as he was in his dreadful suppositions. His face drained of colour, he felt feeble and tired, and the melange of anger, worry, and jealousy consuming him hollowed out a cavity in his heart. By the time they reached their destination, he was in a truly nightmarish state. His love for Sa'iba had not weakened; indeed, as his doubts in her grew so did his feelings—his longing and his tenderness—and all of it magnified his condition of utter misery, a lost man wandering through unknown parts.

Lutfi had barely entered the travellers' hostel and given some quick attention to the state of his clothes when a messenger arrived from the State-appointed local town headman, summoning him. He responded at once and was promptly handed an order formally requesting, on behalf of the Police, that he assume direction of them, taking charge immediately of their movements. The town had seen recurring incidents of theft and a breakdown in security, and the situation demanded strong surveillance and precise measures. Lutfi went to work, exerting himself to fulfil this mission that had been assigned to him, labouring through the daylight hours and into the evenings to improve the local security situation and to dedicate his due attention to this responsibility vested in him. But his energies derived also from a compelling desire to drive away the worries that had so completely taken possession of him.

11

We leave Lutfi absorbed in his mission to improve the quality of public security in this town, conducting himself with honour and openness, ever cordial and sympathetic to those he was entrusted to lead. We return to Sa'iba, whom we left in a most troubled and painful condition, Soraya at her bedside, trying to comfort her and pouring onto her wounded heart the balm of diversion and sympathy together.

With unceasing exertions and great patience, Soraya was able finally to persuade Sa'iba to submit herself to God's judgement and to trust to His divine decree. Sa'iba managed to regain some of her resolve, as she forced herself to acquiesce in her sister's words of solace. But that night her sleep was particularly troubled. In her dreams she saw Lutfi, frenzied, upbraiding and reproaching her with reminders of the sacred vows and solemn promises between them. In her dream, Lutfi accused her of playing those promises like songs. It was her fault, he said, that a raw girlie-boy like Farid had felt encouraged to think that he might share her life.

When Sa'iba awoke the next morning, her chest felt chokingly heavy and her eyelids were wet. As she opened her eyes, morning was breaking. Threads of light were slinking through the wooden lattices* that shaded the street-side windows from view, to fall against the wardrobe mirror and thence to be reflected back onto her bed. She stared into the mirror. Even in her agitated state, she was nonplussed at the sight that met her. It distressed her to see the obvious effects that these recent woes had had on the lineaments of her face, on her colour, and even on her eyes. She went over to a window overlooking the garden. She rested her head on her hand, brushing her golden veil of hair back from her face. She resigned herself to the tears that would inevitably reappear on this morning; indeed they already glistened on her eyelashes. The tears welled up, dropped heavily onto her skin and rolled down to her neck like so many scattered pearls; or like crystalline beads of the water of life falling across skin so purely white that it would put the purest water to shame—skin so translucent that it would expose the most perfect pearl as but a sorry imitation. The red nightgown she wore was open, cut low over her bosom; the bodice was embroidered in the golden hues of early morning, blending with the locks of hair tumbling all the way to her wrists and curling around them like bracelets braided with threads of gold. She pressed one hand to her heart, her palm rising and falling with every heavy heartbeat. Woeful she might be, but she was the very picture of beauty.

Although it was very early in the day, Soraya had already gone out into the garden to pick flowers—the ones that pleased her best and that Sa'iba was fond of, too. She flitted from one flowering shrub to another, one bloom to the next, like a bee hard at work, humming a plaintive little song of separation and farewell. When she reached the patch directly opposite to Sa'iba's room, she could feel herself being pulled in that direction. She could hear a thread of sound—a series of faint moans. As she caught sight of Sa'iba's face at the window, her knees all but buckled beneath her. How could they not give way when faced with the beauty of that image, so deserving of humble acknowledgement?

Shall I bring you some flowers? she called out. These—you love them. I can make you a little crown. Just a moment ago I saw a new growth of lilies of the valley, your very favourites.

No, my dear. I promised myself, that ever since *that day* I would not have lilies on my person.

Now perk up and have some patience! You know well that it is patience that lifts our griefs from us and helps us to forget our tribulations. No matter what a body encounters in life—whatever fate, whatever ill sorts, treacheries and miseries—if a person lets these things affect her deeply, or acquiesces in them, then such miseries will have the upper hand always. Forget your worries, for forgetting is a kind of remedy. It is salutary in illnesses of the heart: keep this thought in your head and hold to it. Let your mind dwell on your husband's fine qualities and then on his love and passion for you. Whatever ill thoughts he has about you have no reality—they are only in his mind.

How is it possible that I might forget, when you know well that my regard for him is nothing ordinary! No, my affection for him is nothing less than the greatest of loves. The greatest passion—indeed it is an adoration that has wholly consumed my heart. I die and live by my feelings for him. If it were not for some kind of hope that I cling to—that his journey will dispel these dark thoughts of his and will intercede for me with the thoughts going through his mind—then I would kill myself.

Forget, my dear, forget! There is no other way. The human heart is too fragile to endure even a small measure of the calamities of this world—the many woes it holds! Misery is a part of human existence that one cannot escape; and it is never very far away. Hardship refines and polishes one's character even as it reduces one's vigour and bloom. It is hardship that truly lights one's way, producing beams of wisdom and knowledge. It is the trials of life that propel people to test themselves, to seek experience. But then, the ability to forget must be the constant companion of such knowledge. To forget is imperative if one is to get on with life, to know any peace. A person who has not been able to forget whatever has harmed them and done them ill knows fatigue and trouble all their life. Oh dear! I have nearly failed to remember that this humid air might poorly affect your delicate form. Cover yourself with something to protect you from it, now do! I am coming in directly, with these flowers for you, and then I shall have more to tell you—more words of comfort to give you.

When Soraya entered Sa'iba's room, she found her sister no longer standing at the window but half lying down, supporting herself on a bank of cushions and sobbing. As Soraya hurried to her, the flowers dropped from her hands to scatter around Sa'iba's pillows. Soraya knelt down before Sa'iba and encircled her waist with both arms, her sleeves pushed upward so that her skin glowed against Sa'iba's red chemise. Soraya kissed her sister—slow, endless kisses—and held her close. Strands of their hair mingled into each other, their faces joined, their hearts were as one. The rays coming in through the window and falling onto them gave their coupled silhouette a most beautiful radiance, as though together they were the very essence of unsullied goodness and beauty. Or they were a lifelike ensemble carved in marble, embodying what the venerable poets envisioned in their most delicately chiselled poetic renderings of love.

It helps me to have you here with me. I have needed someone to show me this kind of love. Last night exhausted and terrified me.

What you say is so very true, you poor thing. The young are in particular need of virtuous, innocent love—to enliven them and to bring out who they truly are, that is, to encourage them to show their precious inner selves to the world. Such a love polishes the rough edges of a soul, and forms character, and ignites the light in youthful eyes. But if it weren't for the pains and griefs this kind of love encompasses, then fully half of the joy of it would vanish! After all, the sweetest part of love is the most elusive—the most delectable is also the bitterest.

Your words are truly like balsam! Whatever may have afflicted me, you have managed to dispel some of it. But . . . when I hear you say these things, I begin to believe that you must have some experience of love and its many stages. Are you in love, too, then?

No, no—Trying to complete her sentence, Soraya was suddenly overcome by a fit of coughing, and her face reddened.

Finally, she was able to go on. No. Except for those who are near and dear to me, I do not love anyone in particular. But . . . well, there are days when I feel as though I am carrying a heavy weight of love somewhere inside of me. It sits in my heart and I do not have the energy necessary to hand it out or to part with it—or even to know to what it tends. Sometimes it grows so powerful that I feel I must love everyone. I know very well how one describes states of passion; in fact, I can describe passion beautifully, but I am ignorant when it comes to knowing it in practice. As Molière said:*

> It all went otherwise for me in love
> And so I create it in words tho' I be ignorant in deed—
> It bows to my pen but if I speak it, it flaunts me
> It hides when I appear, and I appear when it hides.

Anyway, we women have no choice but to submit ourselves to patience—the steed of the weak. Now—Sa'iba, in your eyes I see signs that you have not slept. Can you not get the better of yourself and get some sleep? After all, a single hour's sleep is more beneficial than whole volumes of the finest spoken sentiments and a great deal of medicine, put together.

Soraya led Sa'iba back to her bed and outdid herself coming up with sweet, gentle phrases and comforting thoughts until finally drowsiness closed Sai'ba's eyelids and she slept the deep sleep of exhaustion. Soraya tiptoed out and went to her own room.

12

In her life in this household, one might assume, Soraya had no pressing cares. But this was hardly so. She lived in a state of constant anxiety and deliberation. Yet she found herself unable to ascribe this condition of hers to any particular cause.

Soraya often found herself in circumstances where she could not help but observe Lutfi closely, though always from within the concealment and seclusion of her feminine existence. To *see* him animated—and always disturbed—her. Whenever she heard his voice, or the sound of his footfall, her heartbeat quickened. What her feelings told her was that if the two of them had not been connected by close family ties, she would certainly have been in love with him. It was this predicament that left her—naturally enough—in a state of turmoil, and it was why she had been so unable to speak when Sa'iba questioned her on the state of her heart.

Lutfi would go off to work while, at home, Soraya helped Sa'iba with mending and readying his clothes. It gave her such pleasure to talk of him and to praise his qualities. She was certainly conscious that her emotions—as she spoke of him—were much stronger than warranted by the usual pleasure that a relation derives from complimenting their close kin. Now, alone in her room after Sa'iba had finally fallen asleep, Soraya picked up some embroidery that she had begun several days before. But every time she settled herself to work on it, what filled her mind were these disturbing, refractory thoughts of Lutfi. She sat there in her room, the half-done handwork in her lap but her head soaring through a vale of dreams as though she could see and feel exactly what Sa'iba had expressed about the terrible emptiness of her heart. But here in her room, her thoughts assumed the frightening shape of an enormous, disconnected inscription on the wall before her. She mouthed those letters time after time, without being able to connect them or to take in the meaning they signalled. She was struggling with an internal battle—now fully joined—between her heart's natural inclinations and the obligations of sympathy and propriety that imposed altogether different necessities upon her. She was alone; she spoke out loud without being aware that she did so.

No. Yes—it is *no*. I am free, and my heart assures me of my disinterest—how remote I am from any *love.* No, indeed—my fondness for Lutfi is not love. It is a sincere friendship, a liking for the man Sa'iba has chosen as her husband. Suppose my heart were to rebel against me! I would prefer death a thousand times over to admitting such a thing. Lutfi is my sister's husband; and so—he is my brother. I *will* suppress this, no matter how much suffering it costs me. If I cannot free myself from it, the death of my heart itself will be easier than—

Her thoughts were interrupted by a knock at the door. She roused herself to open it. Umm Sa'iba came in, her maternal anxiety obvious.

What is the matter with Sa'iba? She's sleeping much later than is her habit!

But she has only just fallen asleep. She had a mostly sleepless night. Earlier this morning I was with her and I could see how exhausted she was. I tried to calm her, to comfort her, to get her to go back to sleep. I hope the sleep will do her some good after all that she has suffered over Lutfi's departure.

I find myself very sorry—said the mother—that we married her to Lutfi. Whichever way you look at it, Farid is superior. Just consider how cheerful and open his face is! Or, think of his generosity—and he is well-spoken and witty, too. Truly the measure of an all-round sympathetic person! Not to mention that he is her cousin and has more right to her than any outsider to the family would have.

Sayyidati, do not let your distress lead you to diminish Lutfi's great merits. He loves Sa'iba, and his esteem for her is greater than his esteem for himself. Alas, circumstances have aligned with the treacherous machinations of some corrupt people to land him in a mire of suspicion. He is not to blame. It is the nature of a person in love to be mistrustful if he sees something contrary to what he considers right conduct.* And how can Farid be compared to him? If what we hear is true, Farid is nothing more than a callow, inept gambler who festoons himself in the comeliest qualities but is seen by the world to show the most reprehensible attributes! He is sincere, or he's a terrible liar; he is charming, or he is brusque and sullen, or he is a bit of a fop. He is the worst of plunderers and yet, he is the most liberal of donors. He scratches at the basest means to obtain his lofty aims. He is a silly fellow who keeps company with bad people, criminals, and sinners; and he aids them with the money he procures, helping them to evade due punishment. And ever since Lutfi departed, I am forever seeing Farid's little boat just opposite our house. In the middle of the night, I was awakened by the sound of his voice, singing out loud. He was directly in front of the house, as if he has made it his mission to disturb our peace and annoy us as much as he can. And our neighbour—she has told me that he is known to be in terrible debt, and her husband saw him on the bridge trying to pawn away his walking stick just to pay the toll for crossing.* Is it not outrageous—completely unacceptable—to compare him to Lutfi, a sensible, careful, and dignified man of good comportment and pure name?

I see that you take great exception to my view of the situation. Your sympathetic heart and your eloquent words do impress me very much! You have stronger arguments than I have, and you are more attuned to people's manners of speech and to what these things mean. Yes, whatever might issue from Lutfi, it is true that I have not seen him say or do anything that would sit ill with me. And I am unacquainted with what has truly happened between him and Sa'iba. Do tell me the truth of it—and then, I hope I may find a way to mend the rift between them.

And so, Soraya told Sa'iba's mother, point by point, what had happened according to the narrative Sa'iba had given her. She elaborated on how deeply all of this had affected Lutfi, so much so that he could not but begin to think the worst of his wife. His whole manner with her had changed completely. He had left the city without even saying goodbye.

Therefore, said Soraya, can you not see Farid's deviousness—he played a trick on Sa'iba by telling her that something terrible had befallen her husband and that Lutfi had ordered her to come to him at the hunters' lodge? This is because Farid is in love with her, and he was very upset at her marriage to Lutfi. It is not far-fetched to suspect that he will ensnare Lutfi in the tangled ropes of his cunning, and push him towards committing an act that would have awful consequences for us. Can you not see in all of this something behind the scenes, some force manipulating Destiny? Can you not see that Farid has evil intentions towards Lutfi? Are we going to remain wilfully blind to the truth, continuing to see in Farid nothing other than a devoted relation and a reliable friend? Those who keep company with evil will themselves go astray and lead others into evil, too. Passion, when it seizes hold of those of weak understanding, confuses them into thinking that reprehensible or illegal behaviours in the service of that passion are perfectly fine; that committing a gravely immoral act is acceptable if it is the means to obtaining one's cherished goals. I think we must do everything that we can to guide Lutfi rightly so that he himself will see the truth. I am absolutely certain that if he truly understood these events, this knowledge would dispel the jealousy that clouds his eyes. He would come back to Sa'iba and they would regain their past happiness, by God's grace.

My heart will not bend to despising Farid and believing what you say of him, without some firm corroboration and more investigation and detail. But I do admire your reason and your persuasive explanations. Never before have I seen in you such strength of mind, such confidence, such profound knowledge.

It is the result of my schooling, which is all due to the charity of our Esteemed Benefactor the Sultan. This was the means by which I was refined. It was this school that enlightened my mind through the radiance of knowledge and the lustre of good self-management. There I learned the sacred duties of Woman, and how she must work to develop a pure, chaste, and devoted self. Religion informs us about humankind's praiseworthy traits and a person's best fates. The sciences tell us how society must be ordered and how a person may act and listen according to the precepts of morally upright, refined behaviour and the reasoning mind. I am not shy of endlessly repeating my prayer that the pillars of the State may be ever strong, and the days of He who holds the Great Caliphate in His hands may be ever long. His overarching concern, his tireless efforts for the well-being and assurance of his subjects, his advanced schools and institutes of knowledge—all of this work has implanted in the hearts of his servants, men and women both, the principles of virtue and loyalty. And yet, what I have managed to secure in the way of learning is nothing worth mentioning next to those women who have truly perfected it! Those daughters are a considerable number by now, and there is no doubt of their great benefits to these lands, for they are striving to elevate society through their good works. As married women, they are raising their children properly, etching on the tablets of their little ones' minds the strong and sensible principles that they must have.

God protect you! How superior is your way of speaking, how eloquent your tongue! Come, let's prepare the midday meal. Sa'iba is probably awake by now. She did not like the food the jariyas made for her. Let us go and make something that she will eat.

13

We return to Lutfi, finding him where we left him, immersing himself in his duties as superintendent of police in a town in Salonica Governorate. By the end of his first week there he had acquainted himself thoroughly with the local circumstances. He learned the locations of the miscreants' safe houses and set up ambushes to catch them as they slunk into their hiding places.* He blocked their escape routes. But he could not root them out completely. They were organized into gangs scattered across the town and attached to particular neighbourhoods. These criminal groups drew murderers, thieves, and hucksters, and the local authorities had exhausted their forces trying to follow and encircle them all. Whatever punishments they could impose seemed to have no effect on these gangs' activities.

Lutfi had not been long in post when, late one afternoon, he received an anonymous warning: a small band of thieves was conspiring to set a trap for him in hopes of killing him. This did not in itself worry him much and it certainly did not stop his pursuit of the criminals. In fact, as soon as night fell he went out on patrol, making a circuit of the remote streets that were not adequately served by police stations or guard posts. He had only a small contingent of his men with him. They were out for several hours. He kept them on patrol until they reached an orchard on the outskirts of town which—he knew—sheltered one of the robbers' retreats. Slipping into the orchard as they penetrated further, he began to hear a rising cacophony of voices as though a goodly number of people were present and engaging in a heated argument. He sneaked close to a tightly shut window and put his ear to it. A voice that sounded familiar assailed him.

Those are my conditions. I don't have a single *para* more than I have offered to put into this.

What you are offering us is paltry! It is nothing, measured against what you aim to get done. The fellow who heads the police detachment here is a very courageous man. And he is well protected, surrounded on all sides by his men—along with their bullets and their bayonets.

Lutfi's heart began to pound and the colour drained from his face. Hearing that voice, he had imagined the first speaker to be Farid. But surely he was wrong! he told himself. Farid was in Istanbul.

The scoundrels went on arguing and plotting and all the while, Lutfi listened. He heard enough to verify that indeed, Farid was among them. It was Farid who was inciting this gang to kill *him*, promising a full twenty thousand if they were to succeed. And then, Lutfi even heard Farid explain to them that his goal in killing the chief of police was to deliver his cousin Sa'iba from this man's tyranny. And so, crouched next to the window of the gangsters' hideout, Lutfi learned, finally, that he could be confident of his wife's innocence. He learned that she had spoken truthfully when she recounted Farid's actions on the day of the hunting lodge incident. Lutfi rejoiced, and he felt the burden lift from his heart—this awful, leaden cargo of worry that had nearly destroyed him. He set his sights on attacking this criminal lair outright. But he did not have enough forces with him now to take out these scoundrels. To judge by their quarrelling voices, he reckoned that there were at least ten of them in there. He detailed one of his men to go back to headquarters and summon additional troops. Then, he and the rest of his small contingent surrounded the place, keeping watch until reinforcements would arrive.

It was a brightly moonlit autumn night. A strong north wind buffeted the trees and smacked the walls of houses in the area, producing a loud din. As Lutfi and his men maintained their watch, waiting for relief, he pondered this wickedness of Farid's that now had been so plainly revealed to him. How easily he had let himself be deceived by Farid! he admitted to himself. How quick he had been to assume the bad behaviour of his dear faithful wife Sa'iba. And then he thought about all of the ways he could now dedicate himself wholly, with every fibre in his being, to loving and honouring her. But how could he ever make amends for what he had done? He had been gulled by the blindness of his own heart, the facile assumptions his feelings had roused, when instead his first instincts should have been to verify everything through careful and thorough investigation before he allowed himself to entertain any doubts about her.

Absorbed in the onrush of his thoughts, Lutfi had stepped somewhat away from the robbers' lair. His face showed the agreeable consequences of this new and happy state of affairs, radiating contentment and tranquillity in mind and body. He could feel his accustomed strength returning to him even now. He felt that his spirits were at ease for the first time in very many days. He wished that his official duties would allow him to wing his way to Istanbul, where he would take his wife into his arms, press her to his heart, and reveal that he had discovered the truth of it all. He would declare and vow that never again would he think badly of her, never again would he suspect her. They would come back here together, to his posting, to live in the shade of God-given security and the preserving embrace of divine goodwill.

As Lutfi lost himself in these happy thoughts, the door to the safe house burst open and the gang of robbers poured out, falling upon his men, beating and wounding them, some firing bullets at them. Lutfi rushed into this pitched battle to defend them. A bullet pierced his middle; if he didn't feel it, he did sense his strength suddenly deserting him. It looked like utter disaster for him and his men. But at that moment the reinforcements arrived. They routed the thieves, capturing some of them while others were able to flee. Although he was sapped of strength, Lutfi was not fully aware of his bullet-wound until after the fighting had ended. He had lost blood and by now he was too weak to walk. His men carried him home and summoned the surgeon, who extracted the bullet, bound the wound, and ordered the necessary medications.

On the third day following this skirmish, Lutfi's fever worsened and his wound began to bleed again. Several physicians were brought in. They diagnosed a serious infection and ordered that he be transported to Istanbul. The nurses attending him had heard him, in his feverish ravings, calling out that he needed his wife. As soon as he improved enough to travel, the surgeon had him sent to the capital. His family were informed in time to prepare themselves to receive him and told they must be ready to care for him.

14

ON the day following Lutfi's departure for Salonica, Farid had hurried along the street that ran parallel to his home. He knocked furtively at the garden gate. Marjana soon appeared. She reported to him that Sa'iba had taken ill immediately after their encounter in the hunters' lodge. And then her master had departed to take up his new assignment as head of the police in a provincial town near Salonica. Sa'iba's nerves, she said, remained in a terrible way. Lutfi had gone away without any farewell; by the time his wife learned of his plans, he was already aboard ship. It had been an awful blow to her. She was beset by anxiety, unable to sleep, and torn apart by her conflicting feelings—or so Marjana told Farid. Would she remain firmly constant in loving her husband, or would she turn away from him to rejoin her first love, reviving her feelings for Farid? Surely there could be no doubt—she should be his, if Lutfi were to take a decision and choose to leave her. Or—what if something disastrous were to happen to him while he was away? Next, Marjana promised Farid that whenever she was in her mistress's company, she would remind her of how constantly he lavished praise on her. She would describe his passion for his cousin in the most vivid terms possible. Marjana went on to advise Farid to select a spot somewhere very close to their garden and to be there just after nightfall when his figure could still be made out in the twilight. Once stationed there, he must begin singing love songs, selecting those that would have the greatest effects on a person's emotions. Songs that must remind Sa'iba of how close they were, and that would soften her heart towards him.

Farid rejoiced at Marjana's words. He gave her a tidy sum of money and thanked her for exercising her talents. He wafted home, buoyed on new hopes that soon he would get hold of Sa'iba. Had he known the extent of Marjana's deceptions, and how adept she was at knowing how to embroider his fancies in order to filch his dinars, surely he would have angrily lamented his own gullibility and would have despised the jariya. Instead, for the next two evenings he approached the garden landing in a small boat, and opened his throat to concoct new love-plaints that gave voice to the depth of his despair—to name his hopes that Sa'iba would come to him now and invite him into the garden. He imagined how her voice would sound, tremulous with tearful pleading and whispered words of welcome. He was so confident of it; why, surely this would happen at any moment! Had not Marjana said so? How could it be otherwise, when he was the very picture of the perfect hero: young, vigorous, handsome, and vibrant!

Instead, on the second of those two evenings, and after he had completely emptied his mental quiver of lyrics and melodies only to be met by no response, he slunk off to the card salon. Boulos was sitting at the table, shuffling his cards and playing his hands. He had been sniffing good fortune around the corner but all the while he rained down curses on his luck, insisting out loud that his shadow-opponent had managed to extract a vast sum from him. When Farid came in, Boulos made him sit down at his side and obliged him to wait patiently until he had finished the hand. Farid slumped there in silence, repressing his irritation and feeling as astonished as ever at his friend's blinding passion for gambling. Finally Boulos had done all that he could do with the cards he held. He gathered in the dinars furnished by his imaginary opponent and lit a cigarette.

At your service! he said. Tell me everything Marjana reported, and then tell me exactly what you have been doing for these past two days.

Farid repeated every detail of the account Marjana had given him; and how he had followed her advice. Boulos smiled, spat, wiped his moustaches on his sleeve. Getting to his feet, he paced the room for nigh on twenty minutes. He opened the wardrobe. He pulled out a set of clothes—a building labourer's uniform—and put the outfit on. Did the disguise work? Uncertain, he glanced at Farid. He saw that his friend had nodded off. He shook Farid awake. The young man started at the sight of him, not believing his eyes. He was so frightened by this apparition that his heart seemed nearly to stop beating. Boulos spoke.

Get yourself ready to go after Lutfi. We will start tomorrow. I have some excellent people in Salonica and nearby who spend their nights stealing whatever they can find and pouncing on helpless people. Come here tomorrow, at four in the afternoon. Before you come, fill your pockets with as many coins as they will hold. If we hope to cure your passion-sickness, this is the only remedy left to us. Here, take this costume, it matches mine. Stow it away; we will need it in our comings and goings, to disguise ourselves from Lutfi and his men. Watch out that you do not say a word to anyone—be sure to keep the news of this expedition to yourself. If anyone asks where you are going, claim you are headed for the hot baths at Bursa,* seeking a cure for a nervous condition.

By the time they met the next day, Boulos had procured travel tickets. They took a steamboat to Salonica. There, they hired two horses plus a mule to carry their belongings. They set off immediately. Three days after leaving Istanbul, and after dark, they reached the town where Lutfi Bey was based. They got lodgings at an inn on the outskirts of town which was little frequented. They had rested for only two hours, or likely less, when Boulos left the inn to meet his friends in a nearby orchard. He secured their agreement to meet again the next evening shortly before midnight, with Farid, in their hiding place. Returning to the inn, Boulos found Farid waiting for him. After a night's sleep, they spent the next day prowling around town in their disguises until the hour was near for their appointment with the band of thieves.

They armed themselves and went to the designated refuge. There they found eight men, all seasoned thieves armed to the teeth. After the usual exchange of greetings Farid told them what he wanted to have done—his aim and his desire: to kill the head of the police there so that he could marry the man's wife. He promised them a large sum of money in return for their services. Boulos had already recounted to his criminal friends the story of Farid and his cousin: how infatuated Farid was; how he had left Istanbul with the sole purpose of destroying Lutfi; how this man was the single obstacle standing in the way of the couple's uniting. After a heated exchange that stretched on for at least an hour, they agreed that Boulos could act as their treasurer. Farid would give him twenty thousand lira which Boulos would pay out once they had proven successful in their mission.

It was Boulos, of course, who had written to Lutfi to warn him of the snare that the thieves were planning for him: and to inform him that they were determined to bring him down that very evening. Boulos had had two motives in sending this letter. He wanted to lure Lutfi to them; but also, he was taking precautions lest he be stained with Farid's crimes if one of the thieves were to betray him, or if he should fall into the hands of the State. He thought it most likely that if Lutfi were indeed to be slain, this company would not learn that he had put them at peril by writing a letter that could expose them as the criminals. But if Lutfi were to prevail over the band of thieves, then surely the police chief would reward him for his good offices.

When all was agreed between Farid and the thieves, they threw open the door, eager to take themselves off in search of hiding places along the various streets that they knew Lutfi took in his policing rounds. But there they found the police contingent facing them and blocking every escape route out of the orchard. And they discovered that Lutfi was here with them. And so they joined battle, Lutfi was wounded, and the relief detachment arrived and overpowered them. Most of the men were seized but Farid and Boulos managed to escape. The police did not attempt to pursue them. The pair of them vanished, taking cover nearby behind an enormous tree set back from the road. When the soldiers passed, carrying the wounded Lutfi, the tree trunk and the darkness veiled the two from the eyes of these men, who had no idea that the prey they had failed to seize lurked there.

When Farid and Boulos felt confident enough that the danger of capture had passed, they hurried back to their inn. They dressed in their merchant costumes and left town that night for Salonica. They took the boat to Istanbul, pleased with the night's events and particularly delighted that the thieves' bullets had reached Lutfi. Surely—they thought hopefully—he would die of his wound.

15

THE news that Lutfi had been wounded assailed Sa'iba like a thunderbolt and left her mother and Soraya aghast. They were all stunned by this development, and very frightened—Sa'iba most of all. She fainted away upon hearing the news. When she came to, she was convulsed with sobs. Her state sent her mother and Soraya into further torrents of weeping, worry, and grief.

When Sa'iba's horror abated somewhat, she began to wish out loud that she had been there at his side so that she could have been at his service then and there. She could have treated his wound. With God's leave, she moaned, *she* could bring him back to good health through her tender ministrations. All the care of the physicians and surgeons combined, she swore, could not accomplish as much good as she would be capable of doing. For hours she went on in this vein, her thoughts in disarray and her mind severely tormented. And then she asked her mother and sister to excuse her and to leave her undisturbed in her husband's study.

She had not entered this room since Lutfi's departure. She sat down in his chair, which was placed exactly where he always sat, and she found everything just as he had left it. What she now saw told her why he had treated her so coldly and had blamed her so intensely. She bowed her head over the desk, her mind whirling and her entire body going numb. Then she was no longer able to think at all. She fell asleep. Lutfi's image came to her exactly as it had appeared upon her return from the hunters' lodge: stern, even harsh, accusing her of having committed deeds that demolished his honour. Then she saw his body grow transparent; a light glowed through it and he began to speak to her, affectionately, gently, apologizing to her for having thought so wrongly of her. Happily, she grasped his hand to plant a kiss there; and when she did so she could see that it was just like a child's hand, soft and small. His eyes were like brightly-lit lamps coming ever closer. She sensed him embracing her tightly. She woke up to find her mother attempting to cover her with a woollen blanket to ward off the chill in the room. As she grew more aware of her surroundings, she came to feel a sense of peace; and she thought she perceived a great strength in herself. She took heart from this dream that had come to her in her husband's study. Surely it was a good omen.

Pulling herself together, Sa'iba stood up. She went into her husband's bedroom and made the necessary preparations, setting out clothing and anything else he might need as he convalesced. She would take care of him herself: she was absolutely determined to do so. She would not leave his side for even an instant. Her mother was delighted to see such resolution and she approved of all that Sa'iba was doing. But Soraya was not in the room with them. Mother and daughter wondered at her absence: why would she keep herself away at such a time of need? Sa'iba knocked on the door to her sister's room but there was no response. She did hear the sound of a sudden movement and the creak of a window being closed. Then the door opened and she saw Soraya, her hair tumbling in wild disarray across her face and shoulders. At first Sa'iba did not notice the traces of tears in her sister's eyes. Soraya, for her part, marvelled at Sa'iba's newly calm and quiet demeanour.

Was she all right? Sa'iba asked. Soraya tried to answer. But her voice was nearly choked to silence by the tears she was trying to suppress. She had found it exceedingly difficult to see her sister so careworn, all this time, she exclaimed. It was distressing to witness her sister's bad fortune, and all of this had sapped Soraya's forces just when she was endeavouring to remain steadfast and to suppress her own worries, ever since Lutfi had left the city. All of a sudden now, the exhaustion of it all had overpowered her. But she was happy to see Sa'iba so well-armoured by fortitude. Patience is beautiful! Was not her own happiness dependent on the felicity of her sister?

Sa'iba replied that as long as she had let herself give in to disaster it had exhausted and plagued her. But now she had prevailed over her own weakness. What had helped her to regain her will was her determination to care for Lutfi until he recovered fully, with God's merciful leave. Soraya was strongly affected by what seemed a sudden reversal of outlook in her sister, and this helped her to surmount her own sense of fear. They went to their mother. Afifa Hanim welcomed them joyously and praised them both for their strength and presence of mind. They spent that evening talking over everything, and relating stories of woe and suffering, until morning was near and so was Lutfi's arrival.

The surgeon and nurses carried him into the house and settled him onto his bed. They departed after giving Sa'iba's mother detailed instructions on what Lutfi Bey would need if he were to regain his health.

When Sa'iba went into his room she could see how weak and frail he was. It frightened her, but she rallied. Fearful of upsetting him, she was determined to maintain her calm demeanour. Yet she was trembling as she leant over him. Their eyes met and his gentle gaze pierced through to her heart, making it skip with the love that she thought—now—seemed truly to be there. She kissed his hand, her fortitude giving way and her tears dampening his skin. He was very moved, and he felt most keen to reassure her.

Do not fret, he said. Be patient, and ask God to heal me. Praise God for bringing us all back together. The minute I entered this house, I felt a repose that I have not known for many days. When I am better, I will tell you all about what happened. It is a strange and perplexing story.

I praise and entreat God for your safe delivery, Sa'iba said. My heart tells me that you will soon recover your good health. The days that have gone by since your departure seemed eternal centuries. But the surgeon cautioned us not to try to converse with you, because it might unsettle your mind. You must have complete rest.

Lutfi had indeed found the journey exhausting. He welcomed the repose that he could have now, and he was very ready to comply with the surgeon's advice. Sa'iba brought him a cup of broth which she held to his mouth as he sipped. She sat beside his bed, a fan in her hand, gazing steadily at him. He slept for an hour and even that short sleep began to revive him. Waking up, he saw that Sa'iba was sitting in exactly the same attitude as he had seen earlier, and his heart was gladdened.

She gave him his medicine, patted antiseptic onto his wound, and changed the dressing. For the first time since his injury he did not find any of it painful. And now he was hungry. She brought him some milk into which she had blended sugar, and he swallowed it gratefully. Sa'iba had ordered the household's jariyas to stay away. She alone cared for him—despite the efforts he made, now and then, to get her to take some rest. But she felt better taking care of him, serving him without needing to depend on anyone else.

In the morning the surgeon came to see him. Examining his patient, he was surprised to see how swift the progress had been. The fever had nearly vanished. Before the week was out, the doctor was able to give him permission to leave his bed and sit by the window.

It looks to me as though your improvement has occurred with a speed that is granted only through some sort of magic! I could not have hoped for a recovery as rapid as this. The wound has closed up and nearly disappeared; your strength has come back; and never in my life have I seen such a swift healing process.

Lutfi smiled contentedly. Are you single, or are you married, Doctor? he asked.

No, I'm single, came the response.

When you marry, you will come to understand the value of a fine woman, and you will comprehend the secrets of family life. A good, virtuous wife is better than thousands in property.

Now Sa'iba grew in esteem in her husband's eyes as he observed the love and care she showed. There were times during his convalescence when his heart leapt ahead of him. He found himself on the point of telling her how he had suffered, being away from her. He yearned to describe the powerful pangs of love that had felled him, and then to recount how fortune had finally served him, revealing to him her purity and dedication. He almost told her what he truly believed—that the pain this wound had caused him was a circumstance for which he ought, he must, feel gratitude, because it had obliged him—with the bedrest he was forced to accept—to fully witness her goodness, her care, and her sincerity. But he did not speak; he left it until such time as he would be completely recovered. Moreover, he wanted to wait until there was a final adjudication in the trial of those thieves. Only then would he learn, from their testimony, the precise details of what had occurred. With that fuller knowledge, he could truly display his love to her and demonstrate how all of his doubts and suspicions had been put to rest; and he could do so in a manner perfectly suited to their mutual love and the vows they had made to each other. Already, Sa'iba had read in his eyes that the doubts in his heart had vanished. He did not need to tell her as much. For the eye is the mirror of the heart, and the power of a shared gaze is an extraordinary telegraphic medium—as the poet has said.*

Our gazes settle the interests between us
For we are silence: it is passion that speaks

Sa'iba was as happy as she could possibly be. The joy she now felt lit up her face and lent it more splendour than ever. When he told her that the surgeon had given him leave to resume his work, and had even ordered him to exercise as much as he could, her heart all but leapt up into the space that her broad smile made. She was that overcome with joy.

By order of the authorities, the thieves had been transferred to Istanbul where they would be remanded and held to account before the judiciary for the acts they had committed. But their trial was stayed until Lutfi could be recovered enough to attend their testimony. The day after he obtained the surgeon's permission, Lutfi went to hear the questioning and spent the entire day in court. The utterances of these scoundrels carried him from revelation to revelation, each as astonishing as the next. Eventually the full record of the entire sequence of events was established; it was all abundantly clear now. Farid's treachery was established beyond any doubt, as was Sa'iba's innocence. Lutfi Bey's heart no longer held the slightest trace of uncertainty. And now, he knew the full measure of the wrong he had committed in thinking the worst of his wife. He vowed to himself that he would open his heart to her as soon as he reached home; he would apologize and make amends for his past errors. He would reaffirm the unassailable pledges that bound them.

As he rose from his chair after dinner, he said, I can see the moonlight. And there is a pleasant, gentle breeze. Come, let us go out and stroll in the garden. We can rub away the tarnish on our hearts with the kind of conversation we used to have. I feel so full of contentment this evening!

She ran to her room, not quite believing the words her ears had heard. Nearly sobbing in her joy, she pulled out the gown in which she had been married—the white silk, embroidered in pearls. She put it on and stranded her golden hair with lilies. Seeing her emerge, Lutfi felt overcome all over again by her beauty. For a few moments they walked silently in the garden, each of them reflecting on the hours of love they had spent here, beneath this tree, next to that flowering shrub. It was as if in every tree and every plant there lived a remnant of their past days. When they arrived at the pond they were met with the beautiful sight of the moonlight filtering through the willow branches and billowing above them like a sea of silver, colours rippling on the water's surface. The sight took their breath away. They sat down beneath the tree as they had always done, their feelings more powerful than ever, bathed in silence, attentive to the pleasure of reminiscences and dear memories. After a moment, Lutfi took Sa'iba's hand in his and gazed at her, and she returned his gaze.

Just look, my darling, look! At the moon, the planets and the stars, in their purity and their light. For me, they can only reflect your purity and your love. You must hear the warbling of the nightingales: their voices are so much like yours. And these pure-white lilies—they are only as pure as you are and as you have ever been. I ask God to give me the ability to make amends to you, through the abiding affection I feel. God willing, we will live long days together, all of them bathed in happiness and peace.

Once again Sa'iba found herself teary-eyed with bliss. About to respond, with words of her own to match his, suddenly she heard a noise at the gate and she saw a shadow-like figure creeping along the wall. She sensed something wrong—some treachery, and it was aimed against Lutfi. There were only inches between them. She called out and threw herself onto her husband, to veil and protect him with her body. The bullet struck between her shoulders. Lutfi felt crazed although he did not actually know she had been hit. He took her in his arms, pressed her head against his chest. He saw the blood staining her gown and dying her hair. The colour drained from him and his heart lurched. She clung to him, crying, and murmured, I am dying . . . happy . . . I am dying . . . for you. She summoned her strength one last time and kissed him on the mouth. She collapsed, still in his arms, the life draining from her through the force of that kiss.

16

WHEN Farid and his companion returned from Salonica, Marjana had pulled out every bit of the cunning she had in her quiver, every trick that she could employ to keep Farid in deluded thrall. She described how Sa'iba was infatuated with him to the core of her being. She fed him words and expressions that she insinuated Sa'iba had said—words guaranteed to boost his passion to a fever pitch. Now he was truly like a man gone mad. No food appealed to him, no repose comforted him, and no lassitude attended his agonies in love. What made his anguished state even worse was the news that Lutfi had recovered—and furthermore, that he was fully knowledgeable now of Farid's scheming. Lutfi would expose his deeds, Farid was certain, stripping away the veil of obscurity that had curtained those actions from public view as soon as the police investigations had concluded. Farid had set his sights firmly on killing Lutfi and then accusing the band of thieves of carrying out his crime. He began to mount a watch, searching for an opportune moment when he would find Lutfi in his garden and could carry out the murder without encountering any witnesses. On the evening when Sa'iba would die, it so happened that Farid was pacing back and forth just outside the garden walls. Marjana espied him from the kitchen window. She waved at him, signalling him to move away lest her master see him. For he was with her mistress in the garden. Walking its paths, Lutfi might well see him. Farid did vanish for a moment. But then he reappeared and scaled the wall.

When Farid loosed his treachery on Lutfi, and found instead that he had killed Sa'iba, he lost whatever sanity he might have yet possessed. He wandered out into the streets of the city, bewildered and lost, stumbling into people, unable even to see them in his path. He considered killing himself to be rid of the awful torment ripping through his mind and dissolving his entire being. For now he had killed his beloved, this person whom he would have given up his very soul to protect—having already expended his money, his honour, and his family. Farid wept and stormed and moaned. He longed to encounter a criminal robber in front of him—one who would waylay him and end his life. His pistol had held only one bullet; he did not even have the means to carry out a suicide. His mind burned in painful confusion. As he succumbed completely to despair and terrible regret, he happened to wander by the offices of the State. He went in and gave himself up to the officers on duty there. Stating the deed he had done, he acknowledged his terrible crime and confessed his guilt. The State dispatched men to locate his companion Boulos, but no trace of him could ever be found. Farid, along with all of the brigands who had been put on trial, were convicted and sentenced to the punishment they deserved.

That Sa'iba was slain in the hour of her glory and her victory left a powerful memory. Lutfi was devastated; his characteristic endurance and patience were of no use to him now. He knew that part of himself had been lost to him forever. Afifa Hanim and Soraya were shattered by the news. When word of the death spread amongst the late lamented's relations, and then far and wide amongst those loyal to her kith and kin, there was great mourning and many tears were shed. Sa'iba had been widely respected for her virtuous and compassionate character as well as for her loveliness. She was buried amidst great sorrow for the loss of her pure youth. Everyone felt Lutfi's suffering. He was silent, head bowed, his eyes and face expressing the enormity of his grief and the burden of care his heart must sustain.

When the ceremonies were over Lutfi went into isolation. He remained so for many months to come. He went nowhere but to visit Sa'iba's grave, placing crowns of lilies upon it and remaining there for hours on end, his only solace the beauty of memory. He murmured to himself, over and over, the blessings he asked upon the soul who had sacrificed herself for him, who had lived purely and died innocently.

He did preserve the vows they had made and he kept alive that
cherished affection. He spent all the remainder of his days
living in her memory and provisioning the poor and
the needy with everything he possessed, doing
every good work that he could muster.

THE END

APPENDIX 1

ALIS IN CONTEXT: A BIOGRAPHICAL SKETCH OF THE BUSTANI FAMILY

We know very little about the life and interests of Alis Butrus al-Bustani (1870–1926). She was born into a culturally and politically illustrious family, and tracing its origins, occupations, religious conversions, and diasporas allows us to imaginatively reconstruct something of Alis's formation and experiences. Furthermore, while *Sa'iba* was typical in being concerned with the issue of family control over young people's marital futures (a ubiquitous plot in early Arabic fiction, Ottoman fiction, and, indeed, in nineteenth-century novels virtually throughout the world[1])—there is a link to Alis's own biography, and to that of her mother.

Alis al-Bustani was the daughter of a family with deeply embedded roots in today's Lebanon. It was a clan that became known for intellectual prowess and cultural production in a time of social and political challenge and reform throughout the Ottoman Empire. This family of Maronite origin hailed from the inland Mount Lebanon region within the 'Syrian' territories of the Ottoman Empire. At the turn of the sixteenth century CE, members of this family settled in the commercial centre of Dayr al-Qamar in the Chouf region of Lebanon, while one branch populated the village of Debbieh (or Dibbiyya) on the next mountain. There, the Bustanis tilled the land—the family surname means 'the gardener' or 'orchard keeper'. A later Bustani, the writer Fu'ad Afram al-Bustani (1905–94, first Rector of the National University of Lebanon, founded in 1951), imagined the reputation the original patriarch-farmer must have had to gain this appellation as *The* Gardener, in a 1925 biography of Alis's cousin and brother-in-law Sulayman, published in the journal *al-Mashriq*.[2] Bkechtin (or Ibkishtin), the homestead of Sulayman and his brothers Abdallah, Sa'id, and Salim, burned down—and along with it, a family archive—in 1978, during the Lebanese civil war.

Alis and her eight siblings were the children of two highly educated people who were active and visible in Beirut's cosmopolitan society, as a growing commercial port and cultural-educational hub. Her father,

[1] In the late Ottoman context, Carter Vaughn Findley makes this point nicely: *Turkey, Islam, Nationalism, and Modernity: A History* (New Haven: Yale University Press, 2010), 181–5.

[2] Fu'ad Afram al-Bustani, 'Sulayman al-Bustani', pt. 1, *al-Mashriq* 23: 10 (October 1925), 778–91; 778–9.

Butrus al-Bustani (1819–83), was one of the most eminent male intellectual activists of the nineteenth-century Arabic reform and institution-building movement known as the Nahda. He was a prodigious and apparently tireless reformer; an educator, textbook author, translator, publisher-editor of periodicals, and major compiler of innovative, landmark reference works: an Arabic dictionary and an encyclopaedia, which one obituary called 'a work no library can do without'.[3] He was known within and beyond his community as al-Mu'allim, 'The Teacher'. Alis's mother, Rahil 'Ata al-Bustani (1826–94), was an unusually (for the time) well-educated woman who, as an adolescent, taught in a girls' school. She would go on to run a very large household; no doubt, Rahil's domestic and communal work made Butrus's indefatigable intellectual energies possible. She partnered in running the non-denominational al-Madrasa al-Wataniyya (translated as the Patriotic or National School, 1863–75) in Beirut that al-Mu'allim Butrus founded, and she was prominent in her church.

Butrus al-Bustani, born in Debbieh, received his elementary education there and went on to excel at the Maronite College in 'Ayn Waraqa. He was a strong linguist, not only in Arabic but also in Syriac, Latin, and Italian (and later, English, Greek, and Hebrew). Famously, his mother—widowed with three children when Butrus was 5 years old—refused to allow him to travel to Rome for further study. Instead, around the age of 20 he moved to Beirut, where he was employed as a translator for the British military (who had been engaged in expelling Egyptian forces occupying parts of Syria 1831–41). He then found work as a teacher-translator for the American Protestant Mission. Forming close associations with some of the earliest Protestant missionaries in Beirut, Butrus collaborated with Eli Smith and others in a translation of the Bible into Arabic. He would translate other works, including *Robinson Crusoe* (1861). As a result of this association, he converted to Protestantism. But as his original colleagues among the missionaries—particularly Eli Smith, who died in 1857—were replaced by others, he went his own way, teaching and continuing to write textbooks and to edit classical Arabic texts for publication. He founded a series of journals that cleverly evoked the family name, 'the Gardener', and his sons founded *al-Jinan* (The Gardens, 1870–86), *al-Janna* (The Garden; or Paradise, 1871–84), and *al-Junayna* (The Little Garden, 1871–5). Increasingly, al-Bustani emphasized local initiative to further Arabic-language culture, which he saw as essential to a strong—partly because ecumenical—society. He espoused social solidarity and patriotism based on a shared language and place, and eschewed divisions based on religious communalism. Following the outbreak of Druse–Christian strife in 1860 (after decades of mounting

[3] 'al-Mu'allim Butrus al-Bustani', *al-Muqtataf* 1: 1 (August 1883), 1–7; 3–4.

tension), Butrus al-Bustani wrote a famous series of short essays that appeared as broadsheets in public venues. (*Nafir Suriya* is available in English translation as *The Clarion of Syria.*) These emphatic texts urged an end to religiously based political divisions, and called for the formation of a society based on common interests and heritage. The school he founded was based on similar principles and was open to all, regardless of origin. Alis's father was a believer in the strength of a reformed Ottoman polity as a vehicle for the development of the multi-confessional Arabophone population of the Syrian territories. Perhaps this focus finds one of its myriad echoes in his youngest daughter's decision to set her only novel at the heart of the Ottoman Empire, amongst Turkish-speaking, implicitly Muslim characters.

Rahil 'Ata al-Bustani, Alis's mother, had a different route to adulthood. She was the child of a Greek Orthodox family in Beirut. She began to attend a school set up by Eli Smith's spouse Sarah Lanham Huntington Smith (1802–36), a fascinating figure in her own right.[4] Rahil joined the Smith household at the age of 8: Sarah wanted to take in a local girl to train and foster. It is likely that Rahil's family was already connected to the missionary community and may have seen this as a sort of apprenticeship opportunity, whereas Sarah may have viewed it more as a quasi-adoption.[5] Rahil learned English in that household: she served as an interpreter between Sarah and local women and girls. As historian Christine Lindner writes in this context, 'Rahil developed her Protestant, industrious and literature-based character, attributes that she would gradually refine and exemplify.'[6] Thus, Rahil was trained into a feminine ideal formulated and exemplified by middle-class, white American women. But the Smiths did not espouse 'Westernization'; and it is likely that both in her early life in this household and once she was married, Rahil conceived a strong commitment to a local collective identity based on Arab and Arabophone heritage.

Sarah died young, and in 1836 Rahil moved to the home of close missionary associates. She taught in a missionary girls' school and translated school texts into Arabic (none of which appear to have survived). Rahil's brother

[4] On Sarah Smith's life and work, see Christine B. Lindner, '"Long, Long Will She Be Affectionately Remembered": Gender and the Memorialization of an American Female Missionary', in *Social Sciences and Missions* 23 (2010), 7–31. On Smith in the context of Rahil 'Ata's life, see Christine B. Lindner, 'Rahil 'Ata al-Bustani, Wife and Mother of the Nahda', in Adel Beshara (ed.), *Butrus al-Bustani: Spirit of the Age* (Melbourne: IPhoenix Publishing, 2014), 49–67; 51–3.

[5] Lindner, 'Rahil', 51–2. See also Marilyn Booth, '"She Herself was the Ultimate Rule": Arab Women's Biographies of their Missionary Teachers', special issue: Missionary Transformations, ed. Eleanor Doumato, *Islam and Christian–Muslim Relations* 13: 4 (Oct. 2002), 427–48.

[6] Lindner, 'Rahil', 52.

had become a Protestant but most of her family had not converted from the Greek Orthodox creed. This led to tension, especially as the prospect of marriage came closer. Her mother, widowed, tried in early 1843 (when Rahil was 17) to arrange a marriage to a Greek Orthodox man but her daughter refused the match. Visiting her parental home at the time, Rahil was not allowed to leave until—their help having been sought by Rahil and/or the missionaries—some Ottoman officials, and possibly a consul, intervened. Lindner argues that Rahil's petition to the authorities concerning her right to choose her marriage partner demonstrates an 'emerging ideal of Ottoman individualism' that had been instantiated with the Tanzimat reforms, the Ottoman state's initiative from the 1830s on to reorient the Empire towards a notion of individual citizenship within a state apparatus governed by a centralized, rationalized bureaucracy.[7] More personally, both Rahil's mother's initiative and Rahil's response may also have been entwined in a rival proposal. For, at some point probably in 1842, Butrus al-Bustani, who had met Rahil through his close friendship with Eli Smith, proposed marriage. As someone outside the family's religious community, this may not have been a congenial idea to Rahil's family. Apparently, Rahil did not accept immediately, suggesting that she did take seriously her right to choose a partner. But by the end of 1843, they were married. Possibly, the counter-offer advocated by her mother hastened her decision. This issue would surface—ironically—in Alis's own life and in her novel.

We do not have personal sources that would tell us more about Rahil's outlook—or Alis's. Lindner judges that 'comparable to her husband, Rahil embodied a complex matrix of American evangelical revivalism, *Tanzimat* reform and modern individualism, with the desire for Arab cultural renaissance, but as experienced by a highly educated woman'. She had her own outlook and activities, but 'this hybridity... was performed in a way that she was able to encourage and support Butrus's work and activities'.[8] In Lindner's cautious reading, given the dearth of evidence, this paralleled the partnership between Eli and Sarah Smith, and 'Rahil internalized [an] egalitarian definition of gender and model for marriage, which she displayed in later activities and relationships'.[9]

[7] Ibid. 54–5. On the Tanzimat, see the Introduction.

[8] Lindner, 'Rahil', 50.

[9] Ibid. 53. Rather than 'egalitarian', I propose that, given prevailing attitudes and Butrus al-Bustani's published views on female education, 'complementary but simultaneously gender-hierarchical' is a more likely description. Men of the time—whether 'Christian' or 'Muslim'—did not view authority in the family as challengeable, although there is no doubt that (then as now) women exerted strong informal authority over family and other matters.

Perhaps the evidence lies in the fictional productions of Alis and her siblings.[10] Rahil's training seems of enormous importance to the outlooks of her children. Not only Rahil's but also Butrus's. Both parents were dedicated to furthering the education of the young, and both believed strongly in girls' formal schooling, which was still a new concept. Butrus al-Bustani had delivered a lecture on female education in 1849 to the members of a cultural-educational circle that he had recently helped to found in Beirut. The encyclopaedia he and other family members compiled would feature biographies of many learned and distinguished women.[11]

Rahil al-Bustani was a very busy mother. The couple's first child, Sarah Huntington al-Bustani, was born in April 1844, and the second, Salim, came along in December 1846. Alis, born in 1870, was the last of nine (over a 26-year period of pregnancies for Rahil). And so, she arrived at a point when her parents and older siblings were immersed in a range of cultural, intellectual, and institutional activities. She came in to a hectic household in more than one sense. When she was born, the family house was serving as the venue for the new Syrian Protestant College (now the American University in Beirut), while the institution's permanent home was being built (it opened in 1871). At the same time, the family home also comprised the school that Butrus and Rahil had begun to run in 1863.

Alis was schooled in a leading missionary school in Beirut, the well-established Syrian Evangelical Girls' School (known in English-language publications as the Beirut Female Seminary).[12] It had been founded in 1862 but was an outgrowth of earlier missionary schools. From 1868 it was directed by Eliza Everett (1843–1902), an American teacher with a long career in Syria. The school gave pride of place to Arabic, and a thorough grounding in her native language would have been her parents' priority, but Alis almost certainly also studied English.

Alis was a member of the early women's literary-cultural society in Beirut, Bakurat Suriya (Dawn or First Harvest of Syria), founded by young school graduates probably in January 1880. Members delivered lectures to the group; some were published in the cultural-scientific monthly *al-Muqtataf*.

[10] Lindner, Fruma Zachs (who has written on *Sa'iba*), and I agree on this. Fruma Zachs, 'Subversive Voices of Daughters of the *Nahda*: Alice al-Bustani and *Riwayat Sa'iba* (1891)', *Hawwa: Journal of Women of the Middle East and the Islamic World* 9 (2011), 332–57.

[11] Marilyn Booth, *Classes of Ladies of Cloistered Spaces: Writing Feminist History through Biography in Fin-de-Siècle Egypt* (Edinburgh: Edinburgh University Press, 2015), ch. 5.

[12] We know this from a remark made by the missionary Henry Jessup in an article on dedicating a Beirut memorial at which Alis spoke. 'The Memorial Column in Beirut' by Henry Jessup in *The Church at Home and Abroad*, Oct. 1894, p. 301. I am grateful to Ellen Fleischmann for pointing me to this article.

(established 1876; published first in Beirut and then in Cairo); in the Masonic-linked journal *al-Lata'if* (established 1886); and in the first Arabic women's magazine, *al-Fatat* (established 1892).

Having joined Beirut's Evangelical Church in 1886, Alis would be a founding member of Beirut's Evangelical Independent Church in 1894. Over issues of authority, this group of local Protestants had broken away from the missionary church; the independent church existed until 1906. Alis's sister Luwiza (Louisa) al-Bustani Sarkis (1853–1923) and Luwiza's spouse Khalil Sarkis (1842–1915), Alis's publisher, were also founding members.[13]

If Alis aspired to become a published writer she had role models close to hand—not only in the older generation, but in her (much) older brothers and sister. Her elder sister Idlid (Adelaide, 1849–1933) published her work of short fiction 'Henry and Amelia' in the first volume of the first al-Bustani magazine, *al-Jinan*, the year Alis was born.[14] As historian Fruma Zachs notes, Idlid's writing addressed questions of choice in relationships and of trust and reputation.[15] The eldest al-Bustani son, Salim (1846–84), worked closely with his father in journalism and teaching. But his most innovative contribution was to Arabic fiction. He wrote historical fiction, novels of social critique, and short stories. Fiction was part of his toolkit as a social reformer who saw family reform—and ameliorating the status of girls and women—as a key issue for his society. His novels were highly critical of prevailing practices concerning marriage. In an oration to the graduating class of the Female Seminary, one month after his father's death, Salim Efendi chose to lead with the aphorism made famous by his father's 1849 speech on 'Women's Education' (or a later iteration of it): 'She who rocks the cradle with her left hand rocks the world with her right.' Like most commentators, Salim focused on women's familial roles and the gap between ideals and practices, though he left the door open to other roles in future, noting the public work of European women. One mark of the advanced thinking of Alis's eldest brother is his expressed hope that men would be written about 'as women are written about now'. Men's shortcomings and potentials needed discussion, too—a strong theme in *Sa'iba*.[16] That this speech was published for a larger audience in two issues

[13] Deanna Ferree Womack, *Protestants, Gender and the Arab Renaissance in Late Ottoman Syria* (Edinburgh: Edinburgh University Press, 2019), 213, 236, 354.

[14] Idlid's text is available in an English translation by Elizabeth Holt as well as in the Arabic, in Tarek El-Ariss (ed.), *The Arab Renaissance: A Bilingual Anthology of the Nahda* (New York: Modern Languages Association, Texts and Translations Series, 2018), 247–60.

[15] Zachs, 'Subversive Voices', 344.

[16] Salim Efendi al-Bustani, 'Inna alati tahuzzu al-sarir bi-yasariha tahuzzu al-ard bi-yaminiha', *al-Muqtataf* 7: 12 (July 1883), 709–12; 8: 1 (August 1883), 8–12.

of *al-Muqtataf* (whose editors were close associates of the school; their wives were both alumnae)—sandwiching an obituary-biography of Butrus al-Bustani—gave prominence to Salim's and Alis's father's strong support for female education.

Alis may have received some training as a writer through the feverish literary-scholarly output of her family. The encyclopaedia that their father envisioned in the early 1870s, *Da'irat al-ma'arif* (The Compass of Knowledge), began to appear in 1876. The final volume (the work, unfinished, did not span the entire alphabet) was published in 1900, seventeen years after the patriarch's death. The *Da'ira* had become a family project led by Alis's brothers Najib (1862–1919) and Nasib (1867–1913) and their cousin Sulayman al-Bustani (1856–1925). (Salim had been its head editor from 1882, shortly before Butrus's death, soon followed by his own demise in 1884.) It would not be surprising if the daughters contributed too. At the least, by reading it, Alis could have learned of famous women writers and intellectuals—as well as semi-legendary figures such as Geneviève of Brabant, who features in her novel (see Appendix 2). What was Alis's relationship with her much older sister Idlid, who lived seven years longer than her youngest sister, who was twenty-one years her junior? Did Idlid tutor or encourage Alis? Both must have been affected by the death of their eldest sibling. Sarah—likely a teacher at the family-founded school—died in 1866 (four years before Alis's birth) of typhoid pneumonia.

As historian Deanna Ferree Womack has demonstrated in her research on Protestant women in late Ottoman Syria, one area of these women's activism was journalism, generally within the fold of the American missionary publications and their press. Womack sees this as an important step towards the later founding (from the 1890s) of women's magazines by Arab women, while these earlier writings focused more on Protestant women's 'theological commitments and spiritual practices'. Women contributed essays, speech texts, and poems, as well as translations from English, notices of local events, obituaries, and the like. 'Opportunities for writing and public speaking as mission school pupils, teachers and members of women's societies helped to facilitate Syrian Protestant women's early ventures into journalism and other literary endeavors.'[17] Speeches at school graduations, published in these and other magazines, offered girls a model of new womanhood while reminding older readers (male and female) of how society was changing. While Alis does not appear to have published regularly in the American Missionary Press's 'weekly bulletin'—unless she did so anonymously—a speech she gave in 1894 was reproduced there. Like other articles penned by the Protestant women in this publication (and akin to many essays by

[17] Womack, *Protestants*, 148, 151, 150.

Arabophone women—Muslim, Christian, Jewish—in publications of the 1880s and 1890s), the speech focused on the importance of early childhood education. Alis emphasized the roles of both mother and father. The oration ended on a note similar to that in *Sa'iba*'s preface, expressing the author's hopes for women's advancement under the present Ottoman sultan.[18] While this was a common and rather clichéd (if politically necessary) rhetorical move, it held real meaning at a time and in a place where women and men were beginning to call urgently in the Ottoman and Arabic presses for more schools to serve girls and boys throughout the Ottoman realms. Other men and women remained sceptical about female schooling, voicing fears about its possible social implications.

Butrus al-Bustani's death of heart failure on 1 May 1883 was sudden and apparently unexpected. Alis was 13 years old. A decade later, Rahil 'Ata al-Bustani died, on 10 February 1894, when her youngest daughter was 24 years old. In April 1894, a memorial column celebrating both Sarah Smith and Rahil al-Bustani as educators was dedicated. Along with missionaries, Alis was one of the speakers—this is the speech published in the missionaries' organ. The audience comprised nine hundred schoolgirls, the number itself a testament to the teaching energies of women.

Alis's only other known publication, her novel, had appeared three years earlier, when she was 21 years old. It appeared seven years before her marriage, to a cousin, 'Abdallah b. Khattar al-Bustani (d. 1950). But the marriage had been in the works—at least, in Alis's and 'Abdallah's minds—for some time. Even the sketchy information we have on this al-Bustani marriage saga suggests that when *Sa'iba* came out, issues it raised were already on Alis's mind in a personal sense.

For the marriage had seen family resistance—much as the fictional Sa'iba's marriage choice was not to her mother's or her paternal aunt's liking, as they wanted her to marry her cousin. In Alis's case, she chose to marry a cousin. Presumably, the two had known each other since childhood. 'Abdallah's eldest brother Sulayman—footnoted in the novel for a quoted translation from the French—attended al-Madrasa al-Wataniyya, the school founded by Butrus, from the age of 7.[19] Perhaps 'Abdallah attended it as well. All four sons of Khattar b. Sallum al-Bustani and Maryam bt. Jirjis al-Bustani (who was born into the same extended family) were men of professional achievement. Sa'id became a high officer in the Lebanese army; 'Abdallah became a well-known physician and entrepreneur; and Salim had a successful career as a lawyer and businessperson in Egypt (to

[18] 'Ihtifal tidhkar: Khutba', *al-Nashra al-'usbu'iyya* no. 1475 (5 May 1894), 137–8. Womack, *Protestants*, 174–6, summarizes the content of the speech.

[19] Al-Bustani, 'Sulayman al-Bustani', 782.

which ‘Abdallah and Alis would also relocate). Sulayman was the best known of all. As a young man, he worked closely with Alis's father and brothers on writerly and research pursuits; the two families would have been brought together by these intellectual pursuits. But according to Alis and ‘Abdallah's son Nabil, Alis's immediate family refused to accept ‘Abdallah's proposal because ‘Abdallah was a Maronite Catholic whereas Alis's nuclear family had converted to Protestantism.[20] Alis's father had been dead for over ten years; whatever his views of the match would have been, they were presumably not so relevant. Her mother—an active member of the Protestant congregation in Beirut—may have objected; perhaps Alis's older siblings did, as well. Their mother Rahil ‘Ata's marriage plans, several decades before, had been resisted probably because her family did not want her to marry a Protestant convert. In Alis's case, it was Protestants' resistance to a union with a member of an older—and Catholic—denomination, though in the same family. Only after Rahil had passed away did Alis and ‘Abdallah wed. It seems a poignant saga of two generations, for Alis's mother's marriage had gone against *her* mother's wishes. Perhaps the marriage-choice element of *Sa'iba*'s plot had autobiographical inspiration, though in the fiction—perhaps tellingly—religious affiliation is not an issue.

And so, in July 1897—three years after her mother's death—Alis and ‘Abdallah were married. The wedding was announced on the front page of a leading daily in Beirut, *Lisan al-hal.*

> Saturday evening saw celebration of the marriage of Dr ‘Abdallah Efendi Khattar al-Bustani to the writer [*al-katiba al-adiba*] and offshoot of the house of excellence and intelligence, Miss Alis, daughter of the late Mu‘allim Butrus al-Bustani. The event, held for relations and acquaintances, was replete with indications of dignity and generous nobility. The next morning, the married couple rode to Alayh for a joyful family celebration. May prosperity and good fortune long be their companions, and may felicity be with them always.[21]

Alis's husband was a medical doctor, trained at the Medical School in Istanbul, one of the educational institutions the novel mentions. ‘Abdallah had then set up a gynaecology practice in Dayr al-Qamar, by then a sizeable city and home territory to a large number of the al-Bustani clan. After their marriage, Alis and ‘Abdallah lived in Dayr al-Qamar for about eight years. Their only child, Nabil, was born there in 1902, after a difficult pregnancy (and also following a miscarriage).

[20] Information from Samir al-Boustany, one of Nabil's three sons. Personal communications, 2022–4.

[21] Untitled, *Lisan al-hal* 20: 2548 (5 July 1897), 1. Translation by M. Booth. Literally, the text refers to celebrating ‘signing the marriage contract’.

Like many nineteenth- and early twentieth-century Ottoman Arabophone subjects native to the Syrian provinces, the couple emigrated to Egypt, where there was more economic and professional opportunity (and, for the cohort of Syrian-origin journalists who famously relocated there, less censorship). They made the move in 1905. In Cairo, 'Abdallah again set up a gynaecology practice. But he was putting his leisure time to use in researching the toxicity of tobacco and cigarettes—he was a heavy smoker—and how to reduce it. Encouraged by friends, in 1911 he founded a company that would produce what were advertised as 'healthier' cigarettes. In the summer of 1913, Alis's husband explained to the editor of the Cairo monthly *al-Hilal* (est. 1892) that by conducting 'chemical and physiological experiments'—mostly involving rabbits—he had developed a way to remove the worst poisons in cigarettes while preserving the tobacco's flavour, which others' methods had not achieved. *Al-Hilal* assured readers that his method had been approved by the health authorities as viable and successful.[22] But the market for heathier cigarettes was not successful. Impatient creditors forced Dr 'Abdallah to relinquish his directorship of the company in favour of his and Alis's son Nabil. The latter soon replaced the healthy cigarettes with the more familiar all-tobacco cigarettes. The Dr Abdallah Bustany Cigarette Company became one of the largest tobacco and cigarette companies in Egypt; in the 1960s, it was nationalized by President Gamal Abdel Nasser's regime.[23]

Alis's older brothers Nasib and Najib also moved their families to Cairo. But we know nothing about Alis's life there, or her social circles, or whether she pursued her writing. Nabil was educated at the Collège de la Sainte Famille, a leading Jesuit school in Cairo. We have no evidence that Alis ever visited Istanbul. She may have; or she may simply have read and heard about it, and seen photographs. Aspects of the novel's geography suggest an imagined cityscape more than an experienced one.

When Alis died, she was buried in the Maronite Cemetery in Cairo, next to her brothers. Twenty-four years later, her husband's remains joined hers there, after his death on 22 February 1950.

Thus, before and throughout Alis's life, her family was intellectually prominent and she grew up in an environment that included attention to imaginative writing. As noted, Alis's elder sister Idlid had written a short fictional work, and her brother Salim was a prolific and recognized novelist whose novels (like *Sa'iba*) addressed the sensitive issue of marital partner

22 'Bab al-akhbar al-'ilmiyya: al-Tibgh al-sahhi', *al-Hilal* 21 (June 1913), 557–8.

23 My information comes from Samir Bustani. But see also Relli Shechter, *Smoking, Culture and Economy in the Middle East: The Egyptian Tobacco Market 1850–2000* (London: I. B. Tauris, 2006), 149. Schechter gives a short reference to *al-Hilal*'s article, which led me to it.

choice. In addition to Alis's siblings, her cousin and brother-in-law Sulayman achieved renown as a translator of the *Iliad* into Arabic (1904)—and also for his long comparative introduction, still regarded as a landmark of modern Arabic literary criticism. He served as a member of the Ottoman Parliament and as Minister of Agriculture, Commerce, and Industry in the last Ottoman Government. Against Ottoman participation in the First World War, he resigned in 1914.

A famous family: and yet Alis herself—and her authorly pursuits—remain enigmas whose context and motivations we can only imagine.

APPENDIX 2

SOURCES FOR THE STORY: THE TALE OF GENEVIÈVE DE BRABANT, AND AN 1844 SCANDAL IN BEIRUT

THE legend of Geneviève de Brabant probably dates from the thirteenth century, and was first written down in Latin. It became popular throughout and beyond Europe. Though there are variations, the story is essentially as follows: Geneviève was daughter of 'le duc de Brabant'.[1] She married Siegfried, the Count of Palatine. One year into the marriage, he was summoned by Charles Martel (676–741) to head a military division on his campaign (it is implied) against the Umayyad rulers of Andalusia in their bid to move into France, which was defeated at the Battle of Tours (732).[2] The Count leaves Geneviève in the care of his estate manager, Golo, who makes sexual advances. When rebuffed, he accuses her of adultery and informs his employer. Geneviève's pregnancy, unknown to her husband at his departure, is taken as proof. The Count orders her killed but the two men delegated by Golo to carry out the sentence leave her in the forest instead, where she raises her child with the help of a nursing doe. Golo's machinations are aided by a female sorcerer. The Count, returning home after years in the saddle, is anguished by his loss, believing his wife to be dead. But he learns otherwise; in some versions, the sorceress confesses. On a hunt, the Count is led by the doe or by a dog to the cave that Geneviève and her child have made into a home. She is exonerated and they return to the castle. Exhausted by their years of tribulation, she does not live long. Her husband builds a shrine in her honour and dedicates his time to contemplation there. (In some versions, she builds the shrine, and the two of them are eventually buried there.)

When Alis was 13, volume 6 of her father's ambitious (and unfinished) encyclopaedia—the first European-style encyclopaedia in Arabic—appeared. And there was Geneviève, following an entry on St Geneviève and preceding Genghis Khan.[3] The story was told succinctly. A longer

[1] The Duchy of Brabant was formed after the demise of the Carolingian Empire in the mid-ninth century (and is in present-day Belgium and Netherlands). The appellation of 'duke' would appear anachronistic, given the historical reference in many versions to Charles Martel.

[2] In the Arabic biographies, Geneviève's birth date is given as 680 CE but this would not be consonant with the historical referents.

[3] Al-Mu'allim Butrus al-Bustani (ed.), *Kitab da'irat al-ma'arif* vol. 6 (Beirut: Matba'at al-ma'arif, 1882), 550.

entry that highlighted 'ruses' by which Geneviève was victimized appeared in Zaynab Fawwaz's 1893–5 Arabic biographical dictionary of famous women in world history, which she was already writing in 1891. Perhaps Fawwaz and al-Bustani had read the same source. Fawwaz, unlike al-Bustani, did not read any European language. The source of her entry is unknown, though she did use al-Bustani's encyclopaedia for some other entries. Both writers may have read the Arabic translation of German Catholic priest and prolific writer of religiously tinged youth literature Johann Christoph von Schmid's (1768–1854) hugely popular *Genovefa* (1810). The Arabic version came out in 1866, rendered by Mikha'il Jahashan, then a student at Beirut's Greek Orthodox academy.[4] It was apparently republished in *Lisan al-hal* the year after Alis's novel came out.[5] Perhaps *Sa'iba*'s use of it spurred the newspaper to publish it, and perhaps this was how Zaynab Fawwaz—who was publishing in *Lisan al-hal* around that time—found out about it. The Arabic translation, Fawwaz commented in her entry, 'stimulates one's sorrows'.[6] Jahashan's description of Golo's 'baseness' and dissipation is perfectly attuned to (and prescient of) the lexicon of despairing 1890s Arabic commentary on youth: Golo 'lacked probity and a good conscience' and he proposed 'that which is forbidden'. The translation's preface offered what would become a familiar template: this fiction was 'beneficial...and in accord with current taste, acceptable to the elite and populace, and especially the young who are at school'.

The circulation of this medieval European figure's story in Arabophone women's early fictional and biographical writing picked up on its prolific presence across European sites and languages. In France, it had featured in collections of legendary tales, including the popular, cheaply published Bibliothèque Bleue booklets in play through the seventeenth century and well into the eighteenth. Songs, engravings, paintings, theatre, libretti—Geneviève was everywhere. (From the 1830s to 1904, fifteen versions appeared in Lithuanian, translated from German or Polish, produced in

[4] Kristuf Shmid al-Nimsawi, *Kitab riwayat Jinfiyaf*, 'translated from the French to the Arabic by *al-khawaja* Mikha'il Jahashan, a student at the Greek Orthodox School in Beirut'. The title page lacks information on the publisher and date, but the entry in al-Bustani's encyclopaedia says 'the Arabic translation' was published in Beirut.

[5] Fruma Zachs, 'Subversive Voices of Daughters of the *Nahda*: Alice al-Bustani and *Riwayat Sa'iba* (1891)', *Hawwa: Journal of Women of the Middle East and the Islamic World* 9 (2011), 348.

[6] 'Janfiyaf ibnat duq Barayint [*sic*] min a'mal Faransa', in Zaynab Fawwaz al-'Amili, *al-Durr al-manthur fi tabaqat rabbat al-khudur* (Cairo Bulaq: al-Matba'a al-kubra al-amiriyya, 1312 [1894/5]), 130. For discussion and translation of Fawwaz's entry on Geneviève, see Marilyn Booth, *Classes of Ladies of Cloistered Spaces: Writing Feminist History through Biography in Fin-de-siècle Egypt* (Edinburgh: Edinburgh University Press, 2015), 301–3; on the Bustani encyclopaedia, ch. 5.

Gothic or Latin script, variously adapted.[7]) It's a fascinating case of a nineteenth-century world bestseller. The tale clearly caught the imagination of writers and readers, whether from a didactic-exemplary perspective or a more romantically inclined one.

More than one French translation could have been the basis of the Arabic translation; the latter closely follows one that was republished (and possibly revised) in 1866 (the Arabic could have relied on an earlier edition).[8] This rendering in French was part of the Library of Christian Youth, approved by the Catholic Archbishop of Paris, and, as such, might have made it into a household—albeit a Protestant one—like Alis's.

The tale could be shaped to highlight the figure of the faithful wife and educating mother, wronged by spurned masculine arrogance. Such is the focus of another rendition Alis could have read. This was a heavily moralistic version in English focused on the devoted and devout mother—and bringing in Gothic motifs—in a book-length narrative poem by American writer Mrs Charles Willing published in 1879.[9] The book's frontispiece is an engraving of a castle in a forest. But in her introduction, it is faithful love through adversity, and wifely and maternal devotion, that Willing highlighted. Perhaps this was because she remembered being told the story as a child, with images 'that looked down on us from the nursery-walls'. The French versions of the tale, she remarked, proceed with 'a touch alternatively frivolous and profane'. Her book, to the contrary, is designed as a charity project: all proceeds, she noted, would go to the Day Nursery, founded to support indigent mothers who must earn a living.[10] There are fascinating parallels between this version and al-Bustani's story—for example, a male cousin sparks jealousy—but they play out differently. (The cousin is not a rake and does not try to seduce Geneviève, though when he returns to the castle, wounded, it seems he may be in love with her. The poem is studiously chaste.) Rather than being taken to the forest, Geneviève escapes from the tower where she is locked up, disguises herself, and goes into the forest. (Sa'iba leaves her home, undisguised, and drives her chaise to the forest lodge.) The doe who providentially appears had just lost her fawn—so there is even a milk-sister theme in this version. In the forest, Geneviève learns excellent housekeeping skills. Did these motifs

[7] Aušra Navickienė, 'How Did the Translation of Genovefa by Christoph von Schmidt Become the 19th-Century Lithuanian Bestseller?', *Krygotyra* 78 (2022), 80–110.

[8] Christophe Schmid, 'Geneviève', in Christophe Schmid, *Oeuvres choisies du chanoine Christophe Schmid*, deuxième série, nouvelle édition (Tours: Alfred Mame et fils, 1866), 7–135. Bibliothèque de la jeunesse Chretiènne, approuvée par S. Ém. Mgr le Cardinale Archevèque de Paris. No translator's name is mentioned.

[9] Mrs Charles Willing, *Genevieve of Brabant: A Legend in Verse* (Philadelphia: J. B. Lippincott & Co., 1879).

[10] Ibid. 6, 1, 7.

inform al-Bustani's creative process? Count Palatine is defined as a soldier and devoted husband, as they enjoy the lush garden of his ancestral 'fortress'. But the portrait of married love is soon overcast by forebodings. 'The gray Elfrida' and her sons are 'a false, base, and treacherous crew!' (p. 28). But there is a happy ending. The married pair are reunited and live long and happy lives; their son, Hubert, grows up to be a knight.

Or, the tale could emphasize assumptions made about women (the husband's failure to trust his wife, and his readiness to believe his male aide). It could display a woman's abiding trust in divine providence in the face of extreme adversity, or the durability of 'true love'. With the motif of the Count fighting for Charles Martel, it could take on Orientalist colouring, placing it firmly within an imperialist imaginary; some versions dwelt on the Count's travels in 'the East', and a sequel traced the son's participation in the Crusades. Though it fits nicely into Gothic conventions (castle, forest, villain, dreams), Geneviève's story also lent itself to Madonna-like visual representations, such as American artist George Frederick Bensell's painting (*c.*1860–70), 'St Geneviève de Brabant in the Forest (with a child)'. That it offered exemplary potential is evident in the titles of many treatments, from the early book of Père René de Ceriziers (1634), *L'Innocence reconnue ou la vie admirable de la sainte Geneviève, princesse de Brabant*, to Lithuanian translations, such as 'Geneviève. One of the Most Beautiful and Sad Fairy Tales. About her Hardships, Anxieties and the Wonderful Orders of God that He who did Good will be Rewarded and Evil People will be Repaid with Evil'.[11]

Across versions, parallels between *Sa'iba* and Geneviève's narrative are evident: a happy marriage that begins to break down soon after the wedding due to lack of trust; the evil male figure; the sorceress (in *Sa'iba*, simply an accomplice). Siegfried goes to work for Charles Martel in defence of the 'state'; Lutfi defends the state through his military and policing role. In both, a shrine of sorts features at the end. *Sa'iba* does not echo the theme of motherhood. There are parallel Gothic motifs—perhaps the presence of the Gothic was one reason the tale was so popular, and perhaps it contributed to European thirst for Gothic tales: a forest that could be either sinister or protective; long and beautiful hair; a premature death, and even a willow tree. Al-Bustani transposes the medieval, feudal, forest tale to a modern urban setting, but she preserves motifs and themes.

[11] Navickienė, 'Translation of Genovefa', 80–110; 92. In 1855, acting as censor, Bishop Motiejus Valančius tellingly approved the book because, amongst other reasons, 'it was purely homiletic, educative and intended exclusively for rural people; [and] that the novella was well-known to everybody and was being translated into many other languages' (ibid. 89–90).

Another source for the novel has been suggested, based on two narratives of an event that took place in mid-1840s Lebanon, retold by George Washington Chasseaud in his 1855 work *The Druses of the Lebanon.*[12] Although the two narratives share a final denouement, the stories are quite different in detail and emphasis. The heroine of this one was a young European woman employed as a companion/governess in the family of the Prussian Consul-General in Beirut. She met and became romantically attached to the Prussian Consul in Jerusalem. In the family's rural summer retreat, a 'menial' who falls in love with her decides on revenge against her, but never criticizes the young woman's fiancé. The ending takes place on a balcony; unlike Farid in *Sa'iba*, the jealous servant intends to kill her, and later kills himself.

Historian Christine Lindner identifies sources that suggest this narrative retold the 1844 murder of the Jerusalem consul's intended, possibly while he was staying with the Beirut consul; the killing affected the European/American community in Beirut powerfully, as related in a letter from Catherine DeForest (a member of the American Protestant missionary community) to George Sergeant in September 1844.[13] The details in DeForest's private narrative display more parallels to Sa'iba's story than does Chasseaud's published narrative. DeForest describes the victim as a young German woman without means but of 'excellent character' and 'amiable disposition', and the jealous victimizer as a member of her family who writes letters threatening to kill her and himself.

Lindner believes it was this Beirut consul who had mediated in the earlier stand-off between Rahil and her family over a potential arranged marriage (see Appendix 1). Given the ongoing social relations between these individuals and Alis's parents, it seems likely that Alis would have heard this story. Perhaps she had multiple sources and inspirations which she skilfully wove together. But Schmid's *Genovefa* seems a particularly persuasive model with its emphasis on issues of trust, reputation, and honour, shot through with gendered assumptions, as well as being explicitly meaningful in the text to Sa'iba herself.

[12] George Washington Chasseaud, *The Druses of the Lebanon: Their Manners, Customs, and History. With a Translation of their Religious Code* (London: Richard Bentley, 1855), 323–8. Christine B. Lindner, 'Rahil 'Ata al-Bustani, Wife and Mother of the Nahda', in Adel Beshara (ed.), *Butrus al-Bustani: Spirit of the Age* (Melbourne: IPhoenix Publishing, 2014), 49–67; 381–2 n.145.

[13] I am grateful to Christine Lindner for kindly sharing its contents with me.

EXPLANATORY NOTES

1 *Author's preface, in Arabic*: the preface also appears in Ottoman Turkish on the facing page, probably as a gesture of respect to the reigning sultan and those of his household; the work is dedicated to the sultan. That this novel's author was a native speaker of Arabic rather than of Ottoman Turkish may explain odd choices of vocabulary in the Ottoman Turkish rendering, such as *komedya* (borrowed from the Italian) rather than the more common *roman* (borrowed from the French, and also used in the Arabic of the time) to refer to the relatively new genre of the novel in Ottoman Turkish and Arabic. In the Arabic preface, 'novel' is rendered with the use of a classical Arabic rather than a borrowed term, *riwaya*, which simply means 'narrative' and emerged, from a range of terms used at the time, to become the standard genre label. The Ottoman term *bende* ('your servant'), more commonly rendered as *bendeniz*, is used in both the Arabic and the Ottoman prologues. On the title page and press, see the Note on the Text, Translation, and Transliteration.

Tendered to the Honoured Threshold of His Most Sublime Highness: with conventional epithetic language—the use of *a'tab*, 'thresholds', to signify the lowliness of a subject approaching the majesty of the ruler—this phrase refers to the reigning sultan, Abdülhamid II (reigned 1876–1909). Deployment of a string of flowery epithets, standard practice in referring to the sultan, also appears at the end of this presentation/dedication of the text.

in this era so well-fortified by learning: as noted in the Introduction, Abdülhamid II was regarded as an active promoter of education, for girls as well as boys, whatever other criticisms there were of his practices as a ruler.

what is due . . . recognized: in the early 1890s, the term *huquq* ('rights') was becoming a leitmotif in Arabic discourse on women's status. The usage developed from *haqq* ('right') as the portion or treatment due to women in marriage, *haqq al-zawja* (the wife's right). This had to do with legally established rights under Islamic practice (Shari'a, usually referred to as 'Islamic law') as set out in the Qur'an, the reported acts and articulations of the Prophet Muhammad (*hadith*), comprising the 'Islamic Way' (Sunna), and in community consensus as documented and elaborated by jurisprudence accumulating through time. In the period of this novel's composition, *haqq/huquq* took on new meaning, pluralized and coupled with a gendered collective: first, *huquq al-mar'a* ('rights of the woman') and then, more politically one could argue, *huquq al-nisa'* ('the rights of women'). (Marilyn Booth, *The Career and Communities of Zaynab Fawwaz: Feminist Thinking in Fin-de-siècle Egypt* (Oxford: Oxford University Press, 2021), 16, 108–12; Marilyn Booth, 'Zaynab Fawwaz's Feminist Locutions', *Journal of Arabic Literature*, special issue 'The Cultural Turn', 52: 1/2 (2021), 37–67.)

As al-Bustani does here, women writing in the press created a fact on the ground by reminding audiences that these rights were well-recognized (exploiting the useful ambiguity between 'a wife's due' and 'women's rights)—while the actual content of 'right(s)' was often left vague. The term was also paired in such writings with the adjective *maslub/a*, 'plundered', thereby gesturing to 'rights' not as something novel, but as time-honoured and in need of restoration. This implied that women's rights had always been a feature of the Islamic and Christian faiths.

1 *the final word of command, and the imperial firman*: *al-amr*: command, referring here to the sultan's prerogative as ruling authority and as 'Commander of the Faithful', *amir al-mu'minin*, the head of the Muslim community and successor/deputy (*khalifa* or caliph) of its founder; *firman*: Ottoman decree. The language echoes the Ottoman formula ending many documents: *Bâkî emr ü fermân hazret-i men-lehü'l-emrindir*. I thank Johann Strauss for pointing this out.

5 *Khayzuran*: lit., reed or bamboo. As a given name, this Persian-origin word immediately labels the character as a servant or more likely an (ex) slave of non-Muslim origin, probably Circassian or Georgian. Slaves often converted and took on Muslim-identified names. Zilfi notes: 'Middle Eastern owners—in common with slaveholders everywhere—conferred new names on their slave acquisitions, taking possession of their identities along with their persons.... slaves' new, local names did away with a remaining trace of their precaptive selves, effectively stamping them as customized, personal property' (Madeline C. Zilfi, *Women and Slavery in the Late Ottoman Empire: The Design of Difference* (New York: Cambridge University Press, 2010), 156–7). Zilfi notes that owners 'often played the poet. They chose to confer—to impose—on their female slaves the names of flowers, precious stones...' (p. 157).

On the names of female slaves, artist, writer, and long-time Istanbul resident Mary Adelaide Walker offered the view that when a Circassian was purchased and brought in to a household, their name was changed to one 'of a fanciful and descriptive kind' (Mary Adelaide Walker, *Eastern Life and Scenery with Excursions in Asia Minor, Mytilene, Crete and Roumania*, 2 vols. (London: Chapman and Hall, 1886), 2: 63). This practice is reflected in the names of earlier (including pre-Ottoman) female slaves in the ruling house or elite households who became famous as highly skilled poets and entertainers, and as consorts. A very famous Khayzuran (d. 789 CE) was the mother of 'Abbasid caliph Harun al-Rashid. She was a powerful, visible presence in the court of her spouse, the caliph Muhammad 'Abd al-Hadi al-Mahdi. A portrait of her appears in the Arabic biographical dictionary of world women (1894) by Alis al-Bustani's contemporary Zaynab Fawwaz (Marilyn Booth, *Classes of Ladies of Cloistered Spaces: Writing Feminist History through Biography in Fin-de-siècle Egypt* (Edinburgh: Edinburgh University Press, 2015), 142). Khayzuran does not appear in the Bustani family encyclopaedia, however.

There was a particular taste amongst the *haute-élite* for 'Persian—the language of poetry and high culture—in female nomenclature', though less so in the nineteenth century (Zilfi, *Women and Slavery*, 157). As a name, Khayzuran contrasts with the Arabic-origin names borne by the older generation (Fahima, 'Aziza, Saniyya, Farid, Lutfi). Significantly, all of these could be the given names of Ottoman Muslims or Arabic-speaking Christians in the multi-religion and multi-ethnic Ottoman Empire, although the characters in this story are Muslims. These are also names shared by Arabic and Turkish speakers: for the latter, the spellings would be Fehime, Azize, Seniye, Ferid, Lütfi. (On the spelling of names in this translation, see the Note on the Text, Translation, and Transliteration.) This suggests, in a work by a Christian-origin Arabophone writer, that the story could occur within a non-Muslim social context as well. Of course, 'Khayzuran' may have been a name given to this individual by a previous owner.

For more on Ottoman slavery, see the Introduction.

the shops (*suq*/souk): this could refer to one of the old bazaars in Istanbul or more generally to 'shops'; the latter translation seems more appropriate to this character and her context.

Saniyya Khanım . . . my sayyida: Khanım or Hanım, Ottoman Turkish title of respect for a woman of elite or middle-strata status, also used in Arabic at the time.

sayyida: 'Lady' or 'Mrs', Arabic term of address denoting respect. It derives from the Arabic root signifying sovereignty or mastery, the masculine equivalent being *sayyid*, 'gentleman', and also more specifically an appellation for a direct male descendant of the Prophet Muhammad (the feminine form does not carry this specific meaning). *Sayyida* has connoted a married woman or previously married woman since at least the late nineteenth century, but note that on the novel's title page, it introduces the unmarried author's name. In the 1890s it was still used fluidly to refer to an adult but unmarried woman. A contemporary of Alis al-Bustani, Sarah Nawfal, sought in 1894 to institute terms of address that would differentiate married and unmarried women, likely as a way to highlight the growing presence of by-lines of young female writers in the Arabic periodical press (Marilyn Booth, 'From *Mademoiselle* to "the Unbored Pearl": Sexuality, Authenticity, and the "Problem" of Women's Voices in Language Reform (Beirut, Cairo, and elsewhere, circa 1892)', unpublished paper, 2023).

the tale of your sister: the novel highlights storytelling—by women, and about women. While 'gossip' was decried by male commentators (in Arabic and in Ottoman Turkish) as the sign and pastime of 'ignorant' women, female authors often presented women's conversations and oral narratives as valued alternative sources of knowledge and foci for compassion. Al-Bustani's novel draws on both the local 'tale' to which the character refers and the French legend of Geneviève de Brabant (see Appendix 2), two narratives of women's difficult navigations of patriarchal expectations and ways that notions of 'honour' were deployed to control and exploit females.

5 *while I arrange my outdoor costume properly*: the 1880s–1890s were an era of change for many elite Ottoman women, as they attended schools and became more visible in public spaces. Clothing practices were beginning to shift, yielding hybrid styles wherein European elite fashion was grafted onto existing Ottoman practices. This generated much comment at the time, locally and from European onlookers; the latter often deplored Ottoman women's assumption of European practices, preferring to see them in what they regarded as 'traditional' garb—although what was typed as 'traditional' (such as the black, enveloping *çarşaf)* might actually be a new and reactive presence. For Ottoman commentators, whether writing in Ottoman Turkish, Arabic, or other Ottoman languages, wearing European fashions was decried as wasteful consumption that bled society's resources in favour of European economic interests as well as cultural imperialism. But some saw a hybrid practice as a reasonable choice bespeaking changing times and, particularly, changing views of women's appropriate activities. Women often wore European-derived fashions (or Ottoman styles but with a few 'European' features or embellishments) in private gatherings but covered them when in public, thus modulating their own preferences with attention to socially approved norms.

It is significant that here, to the contrary, Fahima dresses for an outing by donning a long cloak (Tk. *ferace*; Ar. *farajiyya*) and *yaşmak* (Ar. *yashmaq*), a face veil of finely woven white muslin, partially translucent. (On the spelling of Turkish and Arabic terms in this translation, see the Note on the Text, Translation, and Transliteration.) These articles signalled an indigenous-modern outlook, the 'moderate' choice approved by reforming modernists. Arab women of this category looked to Ottoman Turkish women as modelling sensible practices of self-presentation and flexibility which, they argued, Arab women ought to follow. This may be one reason why al-Bustani chose to portray Ottoman Turkish rather than Arab women in her novel. Such covering practices made it possible for women to exercise more freedom of movement, such as the outing described here, without being seen as departing from acceptable social/spatial norms. Visiting Istanbul in the early 1890s, Max Müller would describe the scene: 'There is a larger sprinkling of women than one expects, passing fearlessly over the bridge through the crowds of men. We see the bright colours of their dresses, white, red, blue, green, and purple, but of their faces little is seen beyond the dark eyes shining out from between the folds of their transparent veils' (F. M. M., 'The Bridge of Galata', in Mrs Max Müller, *Letters from Constantinople* (London: Longmans, Green, and Co., 1897), 10–22; 12–13). Fahima's dressing practice is consistent with the arrangement and furnishings of her home, described below.

Amongst contemporary scholarly works on this topic see: Mary Roberts, *Intimate Outsiders: The Harem in Ottoman and Orientalist Art and Travel Literature* (Durham, NC: Duke University Press, 2007); Nancy

Micklewright, 'Tracing the Transformations in Women's Dress in 19th-Century Istanbul', *Dress. The Annual Journal of the Costume Society of America* 13 (1987), 33–43; Soraya Faroqhi, 'Women in the Ottoman World: Mid-18th to Early 20th Century', in Suad Joseph (gen. ed.), *Encyclopedia of Women in Islamic Cultures*, vol. 1: *Methodologies, Paradigms and Sources* (Leiden: Brill, 2003), 153–63; Elizabeth B. Frierson, 'Cheap and Easy: The Creation of Consumer Culture in Late Ottoman Society', in Donald Quataert (ed.), *Consumption Studies and the History of the Ottoman Empire, 1550–1922* (Albany: State University of New York Press, 2000), 243–60. Roberts discusses the Ottoman painter Osman Hamdi Bey as depicting these shifting practices approvingly.

And so, here we leave Saniyya alone: the early Arabic novel (1850s–1914) often resorted to a diegetic external narrator, an intrusive author-figure. This gestured to the figure of the oral storyteller as overt manipulator of the text, a persona familiar to readers of the time. But it also displays the newness of the genre, where authors were experimenting with strategies of time, place, and displacement, and figuring out how to sequence the plot events and characters' comings and goings.

Binbashi... Faridun Bey: Ottoman Turkish *binbaşı*; in the Arabic text, *bikbashi* (in Ottoman spelling, *k* ك represented the sound of *n*, later spelled as *n*). An Ottoman military rank equivalent to 'major'—in other words, a mid-level officer rank. In an article on Ottoman ranks and titles in the Arabic Cairo-based monthly *al-Hilal*, *bikbashi* is translated as 'major', just below lieutenant colonel ('Bab al-su'al wa-al-iqtirah: al-Manasib wa-al-rutab wa-al-alqab 'inda al-ifranj', *al-Hilal* 2: 12 (15 February 1894), 370–6; 376). A *yuzbaşı* ('captain') would command one hundred soldiers; a *binbaşı* would have jurisdiction over one thousand (Méropi Anastassiodou-Dumont, *Salonique, 1830–1912. Une ville ottomane à l'âge des Réformes* (Leiden: Brill, 1997), 342–3). *Binbaşı* comes fifth in a ranked list of the ten official ranks in the Ottoman military in the period of Abdülhamid II.

Bey (or Bek, as it is spelled in the Arabic throughout; cf. the Ottoman spelling بك Beğ, Bey) was an honorific title, in rank below Paşa (Ar. basha, Anglicized as pasha). Particular military ranks were associated with these titles: Pasha, Bey, Efenidi, and Ağa. Faridun was probably fairly senior in the military hierarchy but not a top official. As is pointed out in the entry on '*bik*/Beg/Bey' in Butrus al-Bustani's encyclopaedia, in this era it was an elastic term; equivalents are given that range from 'prince' to 'monsieur'; it is 'a title of distinction applied to the sons of the elite or individuals of first rank amongst officials... and possibly others not of high official rank, especially in Syria, as a mark of honour.... it used to be more specific and select than it is now' (Butrus al-Bustani, *Kitab da'irat al-ma'arif* vol. 5 (Beirut: Matba'at al-ma'arif, 1881), 529–30). Lucy Garnett, observing Turkish usages in her 1904 book, described *Bey* as applying to 'high government officials, colonels, distinguished persons and their sons'; but also noted that the appellations *Bey* and *Effendi* (which she glosses as 'monsieur') 'unlike Pasha—are merely conventional designations as indefinite as our Esquire' (Lucy M. J. Garnett, *Turkish Life in Town and Country* (London: George Newnes Ltd., n. d. [1904]), 4).

5 *near the Bosphorus*: the Bosphorus is one of the magnificent waterways around which the city was built. Al-Bustani is writing this for Arabophone readers, not all of whom would know Istanbul first-hand, but who would probably know that residing near the Bosphorus was an indication of a privileged financial position and social-occupational status. The *haute-élite* built *konak*s along the water (or *yalıs*, also signifying large homes but more associated with a semi-rural setting; the Bosphorus coast was in transition, as a suburban area, in this period). The families in this story represent an upper-middle stratum sustained by the growing availability of positions, particularly for Muslim Ottomans, in the rapidly expanding civil service and military bureaucracy arising from the Tanzimat ('Orderings'), the Ottoman state-led modernization programme first laid out in an 1839 state decree. This led to a proliferating set of administrative and legislative reforms, and instituted notions of individual citizenship—and which had its origins in earlier recognitions of the need for reform in face of European encroachments (political, economic, and military). These characters are not members of the wealthiest class, who would have been more likely to inhabit large *konak*s. The family residence is 'near' [*qariban*] the Bosphorus rather than 'on' it.

The family homes are situated in elite areas but they are not described as enormous, nor are they European-style structures. Zeynep Celik describes the upper-class *konak* as chambers clustered around a spacious central hall. Some, she notes, had 'western-style facades' and—as in this story—large gardens (Zeynep Çelik, *The Remaking of Istanbul: Portrait of an Ottoman City in the Nineteenth Century* (Seattle: University of Washington Press, 1986), 137). Al-Bustani is careful to place her characters in dwellings of a traditional layout and appearance.

in the sublime city of Istanbul: 'sublime city', translating Astana al-'ulya ('Istanbul the high'), might echo a specific reference to the seat of governance/the sultan, usually in Ottoman referred to as *Darü l-hilafeti l-ulya* (the sublime abode of the caliphate) or something similar. (In this period, the sultan's actual residence had moved to the opposite shore.) Often, as here, Astana al-'ulya referred to the broader urban fabric: the old city around and to the west of the Topkapı Palace, but also the areas across the Golden Horn. If the family's residence is 'on the Bosphorus'—and since Faridun Bey was an officer in the state military apparatus, given the location of the Military Academy and barracks (see below)—it is likely that they lived on the northern side, and this may be a signal to the knowing reader that this is a modern bourgeois family. But this and other descriptions may also suggest that al-Bustani was deploying a rather vague sense of Istanbul geography by referring to Astana al-'ulya and the Bosphorus shoreline in the same sentence.

6 *low banquettes and simple divans*: these are traditional furnishings. The household is portrayed as combining a modest but comfortable and

capacious set of spaces with familiar (rather than newly imported) furnishings. The vases are of local ceramic material rather than (imported) fine china (*siniyya*). To place such decorative items on shelves in niches was typical—as described, for instance, in Lucy Garnett's portrayal of the home of a well-off but not *haute-élite* family (*Turkish Life*, ch. 2). The home exudes good taste.

Based on photography from the period, art historian Nancy Micklewright notes the gradual changes in domestic interiors in the second half of the nineteenth century, but also that the furnishings placed by photographers for studio photographs of 'interiors' differed markedly from those of Ottoman homes (Nancy Micklewright, 'Harem/House/Set: Domestic Interiors in Photography from the Late Ottoman World', in Marilyn Booth (ed.), *Harem Histories: Envisioning Places and Living Spaces* (Durham, NC: Duke University Press, 2010), 239–60). The described home conforms to this distinction. Historian Meropi Anastassiodou's precise and fascinating excavation of juridical documents in Salonica concerning the heritable legacies of a range of the population demonstrates the gradual introduction of European taste and manufactures into elite and (more slowly) middle-strata homes in the Ottoman city of Salonica. Earlier in the century—and for a longer period amongst the middle strata—furnishings were 'simple' and 'austere', comprising low seats, divans, large cushions and carpets. But by the 1890s, with the enormous growth in middle- and upper-rank state positions, 'traces' of the new (which were already evident in the homes of merchants and financiers, many of them Greek, Armenian, or Jewish) appear: higher tables and chairs for dining *à l'européenne*, *armoires* rather than the traditional chests, mirrors, armchairs and sofas (Anastassiadou, *Salonique*, chs. 11–12). That al-Bustani explicitly describes this household as characterized by the older furnishings is significant. The modernity of these educated and mobile women characters, juxtaposed with their dress practices and home decor, surely made the point to al-Bustani's first readers that modernity does not equate to European mimicry.

an excellent manager... the schools of Istanbul: household management (Ar. *tadbir al-manzil*), originally a translation of a Greek term and signifying something like 'political economy'. The term is found in medieval Arabic ethics texts, where it specifically describes a male householder's oversight of his often large household. *Tadbir al-manzil* emerged (in Ottoman Turkish as well as Arabic discourse) as a nineteenth-century leitmotif signalling the core of the ideal (urban, middle-stratum, or elite) woman and posited by commentators as the central educational content and goal of schooling for girls. The concept—and the discourse surrounding it—paralleled rhetorical and curricular emphases concerning female education in other parts of the world; in the periodical presses of Istanbul, Salonica, Cairo, Beirut, and elsewhere, reference was often made to the educated European or American woman as a consummate home manager. But for reformists (of any faith background or ethnicity in the Empire), this model was a local one, premising ideal womanhood on a concept of

Ottoman belonging and loyalty, and interlaced with the local ideal of the middling to elite household with its norms and spaces of gender separation (except amongst close family members).

Fahima is named as a school graduate; she would have been a member of the first generation of girls to benefit from attending school (as opposed to education at home by a tutor, a longstanding practice in many elite households, and continued in the nineteenth century, often with the hiring of European governesses who taught girls French and other accomplishments). As signalled in the preface, al-Bustani's novel espouses and celebrates the role of girls' schooling in shaping this domestic ideal: the domestically centred woman who, however, moves through public space, is a judicious manager and consumer, and links concern for her family with attention to the needs of the state. This motherhood-based functionality of female education is strongly evident in official and public discourse, in Arabic and in Ottoman Turkish, from the 1840s and pervasively in the period in which al-Bustani's novel is set.

While many Ottoman females (including those in the Arabophone provinces of the empire) were schooled in establishments founded by minority communities or missionaries from the first half of the nineteenth century, increasingly the Ottoman state was called upon to establish schools that would focus on Ottoman Turkish, Arabic, and Islamic training. In 1858 the first *rüşdiye* or advanced primary school for girls (as opposed to the traditional *kuttab* or Qur'an-based school for girls and boys) in Istanbul was begun, and in the 1880s, girls' schools in provincial cities existed. A teacher training college to train female teachers accepted its first students in 1870. The momentum on schooling was accompanied by an official and proliferating public discourse on girls' education as conducive to successful marriages and public virtue (Faroqhi, 'Women', 159). On female education, see Elizabeth Frierson, 'Unimagined Communities: Women and Education in the Late-Ottoman Empire, 1876–1909', *Critical Matrix* 9: 2 (1995), 55–90; Selçuk Akşin Somel, *The Modernization of Public Education in the Ottoman Empire, 1839–1908: Islamization, Autocracy, and Discipline* (Leiden: Brill, 2001), 56–7, 185. Similar developments were taking place in Arabophone-majority provinces of the empire, notably Egypt. See Booth, *Career*, ch. 7; for further references to scholarship on girls' schooling there, 286n. From the 1860s, a periodical press directed at female readers began to emerge in Ottoman Turkish; the first women's magazine in Arabic appeared in 1892, shortly after the publication of al-Bustani's novel.

6 *jariya* (Tk. *cariye*, both pronounced *jaariya*): female slave, servitor, or concubine, also sometimes used in the nineteenth century, at least in Arabic, to mean simply 'young woman', as in an 1879 Arabic schoolbook for girls (Booth, 'Translating Pedagogy: A French Conduct Manual for Egyptian Girls' Schools, 1879' (unpublished paper, 2023)). Here, it has the more specific meaning of female household servant or (ex?)slave. Selling slaves was abolished in the Ottoman Empire in 1877, and slaves

had the right to request manumission. However, many stayed on in the elite households where they had grown up and had been educated, as will be seen in the case of another *jariya* in the novel, Marjana.

7 *Defterdar*: literally, record keeper or registrar (*defter* [Ar. *daftar*]: notebook or ledger). In Egypt, *daftardar* or, colloquially, *diftirdar*, was the title of the Minister of Finance, following the Ottoman title for the same post (until 1837). *Daftarkhana* referred to 'archives' or a public records office. Butrus al-Bustani's Arabic dictionary, published in Ottoman Lebanon in 1870, defines *daftardar* as 'keeper of the *daftar* and supervisor of income and outflow in the government administration' (al-Mu'allim Butrus al-Bustani, *Muhit al-muhit: Qamus mutawwal lil-lugha al-'arabiyya*, facsimile edn. (Beirut: Maktabat Lubnan, 1977, 1983), 284). In the Ottoman Empire, a provincial treasurer was a *defterdar*, and was one of the most senior officials in the province. If Sa'iba's father was the provincial treasurer of the entire Salonica governorate, this would have been a high position involving significant mediation between the central government in Istanbul and the province's governor and local landowners, who were not always in accord, not to mention the city's merchant and banking families (Mark Mazower, *Salonica, City of Ghosts: Christians, Muslims and Jews 1430–1950* (London: Harper Perennial, 2004), 54, 174, 242; on governor–landowner relations, 150–2).

Governorate of Salonica: the vilayet, or governorate, of Salonica, divided into four sancaks (Salonica, Serres, Drama, and the island of Thasos), bordered on the Aegean Sea. It comprised parts of what is now Greek Macedonia and Bulgaria's Pirin Macedonia. Anchored by the ancient city of Salonika (today's Thessaloniki, Greece's second-largest city), this large European province of the Ottoman Empire became an important international commercial port and hub, partly due to its rich agricultural hinterland and because of its position as a gateway to the rest of Europe, for it 'guarded the most accessible land route from the Mediterranean up into the Balkans and central Europe' (Mazower, *Salonica*, 17). There was a settlement on the site of the modern port as early as 316 BCE; the city was already a flourishing port and area when it passed from Byzantine into Ottoman hands in 1430 CE. There it largely remained until its dissolution after the Balkan Wars; in 1913, the European powers apportioned the territory between the Kingdoms of Greece and Serbia, and the Tsardom of Bulgaria. In the nineteenth century, as a multi-ethnic province and city that had long drawn incomers (including refugees from war and oppression), Salonica was an economically valuable and culturally vibrant region. It compelled the rulers' concern for these reasons but also because it was a hub of political tensions; public security was a perennial issue. Salonica hosted a large and visible contingent of the Ottoman military, strategically posed as the city was, and of pivotal significance in the Greek war of independence, Russian incursions on Ottoman territory, and rising ethnic-nationalist movements (Bulgarian, Greek) in Macedonia—and hence, to the Ottoman loss of territory in the decades preceding al-Bustani's fiction.

(For more on the city's and province's security situation as portrayed in the novel, see note to p. 36.)

7 *sister... a constant companion*: milk siblings—babies nursed by the same woman—were considered kin, a norm that held across the society and spanned religious affiliations. For an earlier period, Mazower notes in the context of Salonica's populace: 'When well-off Muslim families employed Jewish and Christian servants and milk-nurses, the children of the families intermingled and the boys often became "milk-brothers", a relationship which could endure for many years' (Mazower, *Salonica*, 67).

income of only a few months' duration: Ar. *ma'ash* (Tk. *maaş*) can refer to salary income or to pension benefits. Salary non-payment was a problem for Ottoman officials and military officers and their families. In inheritance records from Salonica, Anastassiadou finds goods that suggest lower-echelon military officers (in this case, a *yüzbaşı tahsildar* and an army clerk) might have supplemented their incomes by engaging in modest commerce; in both cases, 'the State owed the two late men—and after their deaths, their heirs—several months of salary. But at the end of the nineteenth century, this was the shared fate [*lot commun*] of all employees [*agents*] of the administration, and the Ottoman army' (*Salonique*, 269; editor's translation from the French). At the turn into the twentieth century, Lucy Garnett noted that late payment of officials' salaries meant they were vulnerable to collusion with criminal gangs (Garnett, *Turkish Life*, 111).

para: Ottoman coin, one-fourth of a piastre. This passage refers to widespread corruption and extortion amongst Ottoman officials, often in collusion with local financiers as well as brigands. In some cases, this may have been partly due to the insecure salary payments alluded to above. See Mazower's description of this situation at mid-century in Salonica (*Salonica*, 154–5). In his study of Arab-origin Ottoman bureaucrats, Minawi notes widespread nepotism conjoined with low salaries of officials in the Abdülhamid II era as sources of tension and demoralization (Mostafa Minawi, *Losing Istanbul: Arab Ottoman Imperialists and the End of Empire* (Stanford: Stanford University Press, 2023), 57–8, 80).

8 *Amongst all of Istanbul's shops, this establishment enjoyed particular popularity*: European-style shops were increasingly evident in the Galata district, but by specifying al-Astana—and earlier, by using the term 'souk' (*suq*), the novel suggests the women are patronizing a locally focused establishment in the old city, probably the area near the Bayezid Mosque. This would be consonant with Fahima's home decor and dress. This venue—rather than that of Galata—prepares us for the character of Sa'iba, decidedly not a Europeanized Ottoman but a local-modern subject.

Focusing on the late 1890s, Elizabeth B. Frierson offers a vivid picture of Ottoman women of this era as active consumers, through their letters to women's magazines and as portrayed in magazine advertisements. These fabric and apparel shops were located both in the Astana-side shopping areas and in Galata. Frierson sees them choosing Ottoman-run (and after the mid-1890s, Muslim-owned) shops rather than foreign-owned dry goods and clothing shops (Frierson, 'Cheap and Easy', 243–60). One (rare) advertisement illustration in a turn-of-the-century women's magazine featuring 'one woman who is veiled in a continental style accords with other evidence that Ottoman women of the upper class, Muslim as well as non-Muslim, were venturing outside their homes to see for themselves the array of goods imported by the merchants of Galata and Pera' (p. 249). A reader's letter specifically mentions shopping for a trousseau (p. 254).

His swagger... offered: in Ottoman and Arabic newspapers, magazines, conduct books, and novels, young elite men were portrayed negatively and denounced for their 'Europeanizing' lifestyles, invariably described as conspicuous consumption. They were described as wasteful of resources and shallow in their understandings and behaviours. While women were criticized similarly, 'late-nineteenth-century authors such as [Ottoman journalist and novelist] Ahmed Midhat were inclined to view not females but rather young men as the most spendthrift consumers' (Faroqhi, 'Women', 156). Such images undergirded a polemics on moral education (inculcated in the family and at school) as inadequate, and posed shallow Europeanization as the dangerous contrary of true modernizing reform. Gambling—also decried in the press as a recent and growing import—is almost always part of the image. Ahmed Midhat's (1844–1912) 1875 Ottoman Turkish novel *Felâtun Bey and Râkim Efendi* features a parallel figure, the eponymous Felâtun Bey (Monica M. Ringer, 'Beyond Binaries: Ahmet Midhat Efendi's Prescriptive Modern', in Monica M. Ringer and Etienne E. Charrière (eds.), *Ottoman Culture and the Project of Modernity: Reform and Translation in the Tanzimat Novel* (London: I. B. Tauris, 2020), 53–64. An English translation of this novel is available).

Such characters have their corollaries in contemporaneous European fiction: Farid might remind one of Anthony Trollope's Sir Felix Carbury in *The Way We Live Now* (1878), though Muslim Farid does not consume alcohol (as far as we see). Both characters exhibit another abiding feature of this cross-societal critique, the indulgent mother as responsible for her son's wayward and destructive behaviour; thus, the figure of the dandy was part of the discourse on motherhood as in need of reform through education. European visitors noticed this phenomenon. Visiting Cairo in 1844, William Makepeace Thackeray referred to European-attired young Ottomans as 'dandified young Agas'; like women in 'harem visits' encountering Ottoman women in European dress and familiar-looking drawing rooms, this seemed disappointingly un-exotic (Roberts, *Intimate Outsiders*, 25–6).

When, late in the novel, Boulos and Farid go to Salonica, they would have blended in—both Boulos's ethnicity and Farid's appearance (had they not been in disguise!). Mazower quotes local historian Joseph Nehama's scathing description of 'the new middle-class dandy'. Nehama's focus was the Jewish population of the city but this was a cross-ethnic figure of satire: 'Soft-hatted, his waist-coat unbuttoned beneath his garish cravat, trousers impeccably pressed, turned up at the bottom to reveal gaudy socks inside his polished shoes' (Mazower, *Salonica*, 238).

The image of the dandy at the shop door puts in sharp relief the women's choice of shopping venue, in al-Astana, which likely refers here to the older shopping district, in the old city. Dandyish Farid would have been more likely to be spotted hovering near a European-owned shop in Galata selling apparel and stuffs from Paris.

8 *turbid*: the Arabic adjective (passive participle) *mukaddar* can refer both to physical properties—muddy, roiling—and to states of mind: troubled, distressed, grieved. Here we have the first sign, mirrored in the physical environment, of a troubled—and Gothic—tale.

the broad expanse of the Bosphorus: the women probably hired the boat in the busy, narrower channel where the Golden Horn passes between the old city to the south and Galata, heading east to where the Golden Horn meets the much wider Bosphorus. *Sa'iba* was published the year before construction began on the Istanbul waterfront. Architectural historian Zeynep Çelik's important book on nineteenth-century Istanbul's urban development comments that 'The waterfront was too chaotic, too dirty, and it embarrassed the order-conscious Ottoman elite, for whom beauty had come to mean regularity' (Çelik, *Remaking*, 73). But for this author, who was not an Istanbul resident, the scene shown through the eyes of these women is one of pleasant—slightly distanced—urban vitality.

Such an outing was not unusual for women of elite background, but it did mark out the greater freedom of mobility that some women elsewhere in the Empire noticed and admired in their Turkish peers. In Ahmed Midhat Efendi's novel *Felâtun Bey and Râkim Efendi*, a boat trip on the Bosphorus and picnic comprise a wholesome family outing (Ringer, 'Beyond Binaries', 58).

European onlookers noticed such events too, and described them for European audiences who would be startled to hear that upper-strata Muslim women were visibly picnicking on boats. Georgina Max Müller, visiting Istanbul with her Orientalist husband in 1893, devoted an entire chapter to boat trips culminating in shoreside picnics—though these were very elaborate affairs, organized in royal kiosks for distinguished foreign visitors (*Letters from Constantinople*, ch. 10). But picnicking was also a local pastime. 'Unfortunately it was not a Friday, on which day during the summer months this green valley is covered with groups of Turkish ladies, sitting on their carpets, drinking coffee and smoking cigarettes' (ibid. 113; also 117–19; and Minawi, *Losing Istanbul*, 43). French Orientalist painter Jean-Léon Gérôme's painting *Le Harem dans le kiosque* (*c.*1875–80) shows a group of elite harem women waving at a party of their peers on a boat in the Bosphorus (Roberts, *Intimate Outsiders*, 104–6). These women and their more elaborate boat are far wealthier than are al-Bustani's characters; the novel suggests that this type of outing was not limited to the *haute-élite*. Mary Adelaide Walker referred to a similar sight in her 1886 book but distinguished it from the lifeways of most Turkish women:

> Neither can a more truthful idea be formed of Turkish life from the gay groups of veiled women lingering in their carriages in the square of the 'Sultan Bayezid,' or animating like moving flower beds, the meadows of the Sweet Waters of Europe and Asia. These women do not represent the mass of the feminine population. The ladies of a very strict and orthodox Turkish household are seldom seen [in such public sites]. (Walker, *Eastern Life and Scenery*, 2: 40)

Walker aligns the former group with 'the manners and usages of the "Franks"' (p. 40), but—again—Sa'iba's aunt and her friend display—in their comportment and their activity—a third way.

9 *Darüşşafaka* (Ar. *dar al-shafaqa*) *School*: 'the Abode of Compassion'. This school was intended for orphaned (that is, fatherless) children whose fathers had been state employees. Unusually, it was open to girls as well as to boys. Its origins lay in the first private educational charity organization in the empire, the Darüşşafaka Society (1863), which aimed initially to train (male) crafts apprentices. With a purpose-built structure in the Fatih district of Istanbul, from June 1873 the school offered tuition and boarding facilities without charge. It has remained in operation for (as it says on its website) 'bright and talented children who have lost one of their parents and who have limited financial resources'.

Fatih is a district in the old city, to the west of the point where the Topkapı sits, and bordering on the Golden Horn. As we are told in the next paragraph that Hedayat Bey's home was located 'not far from' Darüşşafaka, we know that Farid was born and grew up in the old, Muslim-majority part of the city and not in the Europeanized area that he would make his base of operations later on.

a measure of freedom to see his cousin: as an adolescent (*fi muraqahatihi*), Farid is permitted by the families to associate with his female cousin, even though at this age—after puberty—females (at least, of middle- and upper-strata families) would usually be subject to a greater measure of home confinement (see note to p. 10). The lives of peasant families and the urban poor did not permit such measures, given lack of spatial and economic resources.

10 *tales of chivalry and romance*: this may refer to orally told epics and 'folk' tales and/or to written versions of the same. Arabophone intellectuals had railed against the publication of cheaply printed booklets containing such material while recognizing ruefully that these were the publications that sold—an early example is an article on 'Knowledge-based books and others' published in Egypt's official gazette, *al-Waqa'i' al-misriyya*, on 11 May 1881, penned by a leading Egyptian scholar and educator who would become the Mufti of Egypt, Muhammad 'Abduh. Such narratives were regarded as detrimental to a sober, morally strong upbringing. This paragraph in the novel thus echoes contemporaneous polemics in the press on the consequences of a deficient education. Across the Empire, too, such narratives served as 'informal cultural agents', as Somel notes

(*Modernization*, 244–5, 250–1)—and so did novels. Youth may well have preferred such means of education over the formally prescribed curricula, often taught by religious scholar-officials since graduates of teachers' colleges could not fulfil the demand for schoolteachers throughout the empire (ibid. 245).

10 *sanctioned practices... separated her from him*: the verb *hajaba*—from the same root as *hijab*—denotes here the customary seclusion of urban middle- to upper-strata Muslim females at least from puberty, based on long-standing interpretations of parts of the Qur'an (which can be, and have been, interpreted variously). The term *sunan* signifies practice sanctioned either by custom or, in its singular form, *sunna*, the example in words and deeds of the Prophet Muhammad. Anyone eligible as a marriage partner (such as first cousin Farid) would not have access to the parts of the house where the women and children lived. In this period, while non-Muslim Ottoman families did not have the same religio-legal strictures on gender mixing, by custom and accepted social practice they were still likely to observe some measure of gender segregation and bodily covering.

12 *the Sultanic Colleges*: these higher institutions of professional training were mostly products of the Tanzimat. The military school, however, was founded earlier (see note to p. 12 below). Founding the professional schools—and the lower schools that fed into them—was aimed at the formation of a more centralized and standardized imperial bureaucracy centred in Istanbul but also in order to fill posts throughout the provinces. It had wider implications. As historian Carter Vaughn Findley remarks, 'During the Tanzimat, efforts at elite formation expanded, spilling over into educational reforms that benefited the general population; yet the supply of qualified personnel remained inadequate to meet the reformers' needs' (Carter Vaughn Findley, *Turkey, Islam, Nationalism, and Modernity: A History* (New Haven: Yale University Press, 2010), 90). Alis al-Bustani's brothers and her husband got their higher education in these Istanbul professional schools, regarded as the pinnacle of the modern Ottoman educational system.

Gazi... the Ottoman Caliphate (Ar. *al-ghazi*): this title, lit. 'the warrior-hero' or 'invader', comes from the Arabic root *ghazw*, denoting pre-Islamic tribal raids and then referring, in literature of the early Islamic period, to the conquests of the Muslim armies. From the early Ottoman era on, it was an honorific referring to the Ottoman sultan; it was also conferred on senior military leaders with renowned battle records. The Ottoman sultan was simultaneously the *khalifa*, successor to the Prophet and, as head of the Caliphate, presided over the worldwide Muslim *umma* or community. By the era of Abdülhamid II, Gazi had long since become a conventional title conferred on the sultan, whether active (or victorious) in war or not.

equality and knowledge: an unmistakable allusion to the Tanzimat reforms, specifically, the institutional apparatus concerning education that emerged as part of this reordering of the state and of its relations to Ottoman subjects, as well as the reconfiguration of 'Ottoman identity' that the proclamations and reforms encouraged. But it also refers to the institution-building energies of the Abdülhamid II regime in education, which were dictated and overseen by the sultan himself (who was not one to delegate power easily). The passage echoes the novel's authorial preface with its praise of institutional reforms undertaken during the present sultan's reign. As a Christian-origin Ottoman subject, al-Bustani also may have been particularly keen to allude to the notion of equal civic subjecthood for members of minority communities.

even in the lowliest and poorest villages: the Ministry of Public Education was established in 1857 during the regime of Sultan Abdülmecid. From 1869 (during the reign of Abdülhamid II's immediate predecessor, Abdülaziz), a 'Regulation of Public Education' spurred—or dictated—the further establishment of schooling at all levels across the Empire. Traditionally the religious establishment saw to education, from *mekteb*s (Qur'an schools, Ar. *kuttab*) for the youngest to the *medrese* (Ar. *madrasa*) for older boys. Now the state took on the primary role. While the novel is set in Istanbul, al-Bustani would have witnessed the results of this activity in her native Lebanon even though she was not educated in the state system.

Of the educational vigour of the Abdülhamid II period, Zeynep Seviner comments that now 'education was truly turned into a tool of government control over the moral education' of the populace—together with the new textbooks it promulgated. The sultan, she argues, 'largely envisioned this standardization as a project of authoritarian-Islamic modernization' but the availability of 'a multitude of choices' in education tempered the realization of this vision (Zeynep Seviner, 'Thinking in French, Writing in Persian: Aesthetics, Intelligibility, and the Literary Turkish of the 1890s', in Monica M. Ringer and Etienne E. Charrière (eds.), *Ottoman Culture and the Project of Modernity: Reform and Translation in the Tanzimat Novel* (London: I. B. Tauris, 2020), 19–36; 22, 23, 23).

the military schools of Istanbul: changes to the Empire's military structure and the founding of schools for military training preceded the Tanzimat and emerged partly in response to a need to reassert central power over warlords dispersed across Ottoman territory. By the beginning of the nineteenth century there was a Naval Engineering School. The next step was 'to create a European-style infantry known as the Nizam-ı Cedid (New Order)' (Findley, *Turkey*, 31) and a reorganization and regulation of the existing military structure or Janissary Corps—but the latter refused to work with the new military corps and successfully rose up and removed then-sultan Selim III from power (1807). Wide-ranging reform was also hampered by financial limitations, forms of resistance, and military-political crises (Findley, *Turkey*, 31–7). In 1826, Sultan Mahmud II decimated the Janissaries, thereby ending the corps' existence. Gradually—and not without major challenges—a modern military was established. A Military Medical School (1827) and Military Academy known as the

Harbiye (1834) were set up: the latter is presumably where Lutfi acquires his officer training and credentials.

Findley notes a point that does not emerge explicitly in the novel but may be of relevance as Lutfi encounters resistance in Salonica: 'Among military officers, the distinction between "school men" (*mektepli*), who studied in the new academies, and "regimentals" (*alaylı*), who rose through the ranks and were not always even literate, created antagonisms for the rest of the empire's history' (*Turkey*, 90; see also 41). Lutfi was emphatically a 'school man'. At the time this novel was published, the Military School curriculum had been 'upgraded' and the percentage of educated military officers increased (from 10 per cent to 25 per cent, 1884–99; Findley, *Turkey*, 156) (On the Harbiye's location, see notes to pp. 14, 17.)

13 *the Istanbul-based garrison*: from 1843 the Empire was sectioned into five zones with an army based in each. Under Abdülhamid II, there were seven military regions each with an army named for the region. However, the First Army, based in Istanbul, was known as the Imperial Army. To be based in Istanbul would have been a plum assignment—although also closer to the infinite machinations and power games at court (not necessarily an advantage), which the novel certainly does not address. As we shall see, reassignment was not impossible. What is not clear is whether Lutfi's 'garrison' or 'military guard of Istanbul' (*hamiyat Astana*) is part of the regular army or a separate unit attached to the central bureaucracy in the old city or perhaps at the sultan's palace of Yıldız, where Abdülhamid II had consolidated political power. And—army garrison or gendarmerie? In his reassignment, Lutfi clearly has policing duties. In Istanbul, was Lutfi amongst the officers always present in regimental dress at the sultan's weekly Friday *selamlik* (ceremonial visit to the mosque)? This was an elaborate fixture described in detail by visiting Europeans such as Georgina Müller. In Turkish, the palace guard regiment was known as *hassa*. The reference to 'Astana' in the novel may suggest that Lutfi's appointment was not specifically to Yıldız. He is based at 'the barracks', not at the Palace. In Butrus al-Bustani's encyclopaedia, in the volume published in 1882, the entry on '*hamiya*/garrison' defines it as 'an army group working in the city to keep it safe from sudden incursions by an enemy, whether [the city] is fortified or not, and whether or not it is wartime.... Armies might be deployed to protect the country on its borders, and then they are called *hamiyat al-hudud* or *haras* [guards] *al-hudud*' (Butrus al-Bustani, *Kitab da'irat al-ma'arif* vol. 6 (Beirut: Matba'at al-ma'arif, 1882), 661). But my invaluably encyclopaedic Ottomanist colleague Johann Strauss tells me that '*hâmiyet* is unknown in this sense in Ottoman Turkish; for 'guard' the term *muhafiz* is used'.

14 *Lutfi Bey... on the Bosphorus*: that Lutfi can depend on inherited family property and not simply on a military salary prepares us for this move. As noted, homes on the Bosphorus were generally the province of the wealthier Istanbullites. The description here suggests an impressive but relatively small and modest *konak*. That Lutfi is moving from a smaller

residence adjacent to Sa'iba's into a larger marital residence tells us that, with this marriage, his wife is improving her family's financial and social position.

As opposed to Fahima's home 'near the Bosphorus', this home is 'on the Bosphorus'. This suggests not only an 'upward' move, but more pointedly that this home is located on the newer-developed Asian (Galata) side of the city, a distinct social move for Sa'iba's family that had been based in the Istanbul (Fatih) area (although Aunt Fahima—married to another government employee—may also live on the Galata side). Apart from the new marital home being a larger structure, it made sense for Lutfi to reside in the area. The Military School was on this side, to the north of Pera/Beyoğlu (see note to p. 13), the principal military barracks were nearby, while the sultan's household and new headquarters at Yıldız were not far away. 'The transfer of the army barracks outside the old city walls to the banks of the Bosphorus precipitated the migration of many elites to its shores' (Savvas E. Tsilenis, 'The Architecture of Constantinople/Istanbul at the End of the Nineteenth Century: The Work of Periclis D. Fotiadis', *Journal of the Ottoman and Turkish Studies Association* 9: 1 (Spring 2022), 71–99; 77). Specifically, elite military personnel moved to the Asian side 'with the positioning of the Military College at Kuleli or the army barracks at Selimiye' (ibid. 78; see Çelik, *Remaking*, 39–42). But as Lutfi is from an 'old family' and the home is already established, this is not part of the nouveau construction rush further along the Bosphorus shore that took place in the second half of the nineteenth century. Again, al-Bustani seems to be at pains to show that these are not 'nouveau-riche' or 'Europeanized' families. Tsilenis emphasizes that the construction boom on this side of the city was 'made possible by overspending by the state and, more specifically, by the court, now indebted to capital from the notorious bankers at Galata' ('Architecture', 14). Lutfi stands in sober contrast to this picture.

The house's location and the fact that Lutfi inherited it suggest (as does the story itself) that he is not amongst the palace-associated elite but rather of a more modest and independent situation. Mostafa Minawi's portrait of Arab Ottoman officials describes the nearby area as a popular one for military and civilian officials, and indeed as almost a palace annexe. His subject Sadiq al-'Azmi, from Damascus, attended the Military College, and was among the sultan's aides-de-camp. He resided in a *konak* with a large garden near the palace—and provided by it—in Teşvikiye, a 'purpose-built neighbourhood for Palace-associated elites' that particularly developed in the 1880s and was 'a short walk from the military college' (Minawi, *Losing Istanbul*, 34, 36).

15 *Recall the poet's lines!*: in the early Arabic novel, lines of poetry were often inserted; most often the poet was not named. Such quotations might be the author's verses, but more likely they would invoke the authority of a well-known poet. Readers who grew up hearing poetry might recognize the lines. These are from a poem describing a *jariya* in an anthology

compiled by the scholar Badr al-Din al-Hasan b. 'Umar [known as] Ibn Habib al-Halabi ('the Aleppan', 1310–77), *Nasim al-saba*. The anthology was published in 1873 in Alexandria and 1884/5 in Istanbul; thus, al-Bustani (and Fahima, if she read Arabic!) could have read the poem there.

Because al-Bustani's novel is less akin to well-established traditions of Arabic prose writing than were many other novels of this period and before, it is slightly surprising to find premodern Arabic poetry quoted within it. But if we take these descriptions as the continuing narrative of Sa'iba's aunt (for the narrating voice seems to blend hers with that of an external narrator), the poetry is not out of place. It could have been naturally recited by a cultured woman such as Fahima, although perhaps one would not expect a poem in praise of a *jariya* to be uppermost in her mind! In the anthology, these lines appear in chapter 11, 'On describing the *jariya*'.

15 *walls of light*: *suwar munira*, literally, 'well-lit walls'. 'Light' was a ubiquitous metaphorical figure in the era's public discourse, as in the preface's paean to the sultan's reformist work. It may serve here as a metaphor for the light of knowledge and/or good comportment—signifying an 'enlightened' person.

He fêted her...friends and acquaintances: gender conventions meant that the men's and women's celebrations would have been separate.

He wore his uniform well... his Majidi medal: following the abolishment of the Janissaries, one sign of a radically transformed view of the military was Mahmud II's nineteenth-century dress reform, with European-style military uniforms—trousers and frock coat—and, soon, the fez. The Mecidiye (as spelled in Turkish; Ar. *majidi/yya*; often rendered in English as Medjidie) Order was an honour (comprising various degrees) conferred by the sultan on valued civil and military personnel as well as distinguished foreign individuals. It was instituted by Sultan Abdülmecid in 1851/2. Following the Crimean War, a number of British and French military personnel were decorated. The honour came with a resplendent medal.

16 *the East*: in Arabic, *al-Sharq*, 'the East', was often used in public discourse as an umbrella term that could signify a pan-Asian or *outre*-European solidarity. But most often it connoted the people and societies of the Arabophone, Turkophone, and Persophone regions, and did not distinguish by religion or ethnicity. Thus, it was a particularly handy appellation for non-Muslim (minority community) writers to use in an inclusive but vague or possibly ambiguous sense.

his precedence in law... or do her injury: Al-Bustani, whom readers would have known was of a Christian-origin family, focuses here on practices specific to Muslims, although common expectations concerning female behaviour and gendered spatial distribution spanned faith communities. The text invokes an issue that commentators (women and men) often criticized when they took a reformist stance towards the marriage institution: Muslim men's easy access to unilateral divorce, a right that Muslim women did not have. Nor did Christian women (or men), although in her study of Protestant women in Syria in this era, Deanna Ferree Womack notes that even if divorce was 'prohibited by the Middle Eastern church hierarchies that oversaw matters of civil law for Ottoman Christians... divorces occurred with more frequency among Christian women writers and intellectuals', and notes a case where the Syrian Evangelical Church accepted a separated (or possibly divorced) woman into its congregation (Deanna Ferree Womack, *Protestants, Gender and the Arab Renaissance in Late Ottoman Syria* (Edinburgh: Edinburgh University Press, 2019), 154–5).

The passage possibly also implies a second, controversial practice: polygyny. The verb *yuḍārru*, 'to harm', is used; a related form from the same root means 'to take a second/further wife' (*yuḍirru*); a *ḍārra* is a co-wife.

This is the point in the novel where a reader might particularly wonder whether al-Bustani was writing in hopes of her novel being translated into one or more European languages. Explanations of Istanbul's architecture and society could be aimed at an Arabophone audience, but here the text appears to explain Ottoman Islamic practice—an adjacent society that is part of the author's and her likely first readers' lifeworld—to an audience with little knowledge of it. Literate Arabophone Christian readers in Lebanon would hardly have needed this explanation. Such comparative polemics on 'marriage' in 'East' versus 'West' would become a ubiquitous presence in the Arabic press of the 1890s: perhaps al-Bustani's disquisition here is one of the early instances of it, though there were a few similar writings already available to readers.

17 *such a sweet temper... a good knowledge of household management*: this sentence offers the era's reformists' prospectus of a good woman/good wife—educated but compliant—as spelled out endlessly in polemics in the press and myriad guides to conduct, which often doubled as curricula for girls' schools.

the barracks: military barracks were located on the Galata/Asian side of the city, not far from the Military School: 'the bare hills of Taksim and Maçka were dotted with military barracks', says Çelik (*Remaking*, 127), and they had a 'neoclassical appearance' (p. 138). Erected in the 1860s, they were a visible component of a reorganized armed forces; in the Hamidian era, several more were built, closer to Yıldız.

> These over-scaled structures that marked the otherwise bare hills of the Bosphorus became conspicuous landmarks in the capital's nineteenth-century urban image. Rectangular, with large interior courtyards, the barracks had similar layouts. Their orderly and symmetrical façades were furnished with a severe and spare classicism, befitting the military spirit (Çelik, *Remaking*, 139).

your study: although the family resides in a conventionally laid out Ottoman home, Lutfi's study-library (*maktab*) is perhaps a 'transitional' space that signals his modernity. Members of the traditional elite certainly had significant libraries at home, but *l'homme de cabinet*, who spent his time in his study, was perhaps a more recent type (Anastassiadou, *Salonique*, 263).

17 *this song*: this is a poem composed by the celebrated medieval Sufi poet Ibn al-Farid (1181–1235). As such, it is open to multiple significations. While the couple's discussion here focuses on 'sacrifice' in romantic-sexual love, readers familiar with Sufi poetry might draw spiritual lessons from it, as Lutfi and Sa'iba appear to do.

entrails: the bowels or gut were believed to be the seat of passion; they are a frequently deployed figure in the Arabic poetry of this era and before.

18 *Ya Sidi*: *sidi*: shortened, familiar form of *sayyidi*, 'my master' or 'my lord', as *sayyidati* is 'my mistress' or 'my lady'. Here, it signifies familiarity and fondness, while also gesturing to the dominant understanding of household patriarchy, the male as head of household. The feminine forms do not quite carry this notion of headship! *Ya*: Arabic vocative, 'O'.

a spreading willow tree shaded them: while plane-trees, cypresses, and acacias were more common to the area's ecology, there are mentions of weeping willows. In her travelogue, Mary Adelaide Walker included long passages of nature description and tree types. Travelling near Bursa, she observed 'the drooping thread-like streamers of a weeping willow' (Walker, *Eastern Life and Scenery*, 2: 134). In the Bustani encyclopaedia, an entry for *safsaf*/saule associates the weeping willow with graveyards ('they are used to adorn graves') which is metaphorically apropos to this story. '[T]hey have long flexible branches that bend to the ground as if they are evincing a state of grief and submission . . . at the end of the year, their sap comes out in the shape of tears, at the tips of their branches; perhaps this is why they are described as weeping [*kanat tasmiyyataha bi'l-bukka'*].' This was in one of the two volumes published after the novel came out: Al-Bustani [family], *Kitab da'irat al-ma'arif* vol. 10 (Cairo: Matba'at al-hilal, 1898), 728.

19 *Beyoğlu*: also known as Pera (the 'European' name), this is a part of the city located on the Asian side and to the north of the old walled town of Galata. It was known for its European-style hotels, fashionable shops, and entertainment sites, licit and illicit.

have banned gambling in clubs and public areas: the sultan is reported to have prohibited gambling *c.*1898, but likely there were earlier orders banning or regulating it, as the regime was attempting to control nightlife in general. Novels—Arabic and Turkish—inveighed against gambling as a wasteful and immoral pursuit, as did newspaper polemics. That this novel juxtaposes gambling and the theatre highlights anxiety about theatres as sites of possibly questionable activity, even as intellectuals also saw theatre as a fulcrum of public education—and wrote plays.

20 *He affected... his limbs*: the figure of the young dandy with his Europeanizing demeanour and habits is often portrayed in this era as not only immoral and wasteful but also effeminate. The emerging genre of etiquette/behaviour manuals in Arabic (often translated or adapted from the French) warned young males not to grow their hair long or to spend too much time and money on their appearance. (For an example: Marilyn Booth, '"Go directly home with decorum": Conduct Books for Egypt's Young, c.1912', in Joseph E. Lowry and Shawkat M. Toorawa (eds.), *Arabic Humanities, Islamic Thought: Essays in Honor of Everett K. Rowson* (Leiden: Brill, 2017), 393–415.)

cultured sorts: the Arabic term is *adib*, signifying not only a 'person of letters' but one immersed in the moral-behavioural model that engagement with classical Arabic texts—religious or not—would impart. The term connotes a formation both cultured and morally impeccable. In this period, female writers who published in the press were often given the epithet *adiba*, the feminine form, as their names were introduced.

21 *This man... mischief*: in popular Arabic literature of the time (for example, dialect poetry and plays in Egypt), Greek men were often caricatured and typed as tavern owners, drunks, and 'heavies', and their pronunciation of Arabic was mocked. (It is true that many of the taverns in Egyptian cities and towns at the time were run by Greek proprietors.) In Istanbul and the Macedonian region, the large number of Ottoman Greeks and their economic, social, and cultural weight might dilute this picture. Yet, after the declaration of the independent Kingdom of Greece (1821), some ethnic Greeks might be distrusted and resented by Ottoman subjects, and they lost the prominent role in the Ottoman bureaucracy that they had enjoyed earlier. They were also *tercüman*s, or translator-guides, associated with the tourist trade centred in Beyoğlu/Pera, and, as such, disrespected by many Ottoman Muslim subjects. But this likely had to do more with perceived class and occupation than with ethnicity: after all, even in the late empire, some high officials most in favour were Greeks—such as the sultan's physician.

Boulos Amin: 'Boulos' (Paul/Pavlos) was one of the names most often given to caricatures of Greeks in Arabic texts (another was Yanni). There is an irony to the name: *amin* means 'trustworthy'.

Marjana: like Khayzuran, Marjana is a *jariya*. Though she had likely been manumitted, many in her situation stayed on in elite households where they had grown up and been educated. This is how Marjana's life is described.

Unlike Khayzuran, in the novel Marjana fills the role of the 'evil sidekick', a stock figure found throughout oral narratives and in the early Arabic novel, and connected to the 'wiles of women' theme prevalent in folklore but also associated with early Islamic history and rhetoric.

Marjana is a name known from the famous story of 'Ali Baba and the Forty Thieves', a tale that featured in some translations of *The Arabian*

Nights (most famously, and first, the eighteenth-century collection of Antoine Galland), having been told orally to Galland by a Syrian Maronite who had travelled to Paris, Hanna Diyab. Marjana is the resourceful *jariya* of the late merchant Qasim whose quick thinking and bold but discreet actions destroy the thieves and then their captain, saving the lives of the good woodcutter and his family, who are contrasted with the ill-fated greedy brother, Qasim. In European versions, her name is often spelled Morgiana. One wonders whether al-Bustani chose this name as one familiar to European readers (given the enormous popularity of the Ali Baba story from Galland's time on, in English, French, and German at least), if she hoped to have her novel translated.

It seems no accident that al-Bustani chose a celebrated royal *jariya*—Khayzuran—as namesake of Fahima's 'good' servant, and Marjana—echoes of the *Nights*—as the stereotypical female trickster-sidekick, even though Marjana in the 'Ali Baba' narrative is smart but not evil.

23 *Devious Dalila*: a figure from Arabic folk tales, featuring in some manuscripts of *The Arabian Nights* along with other 'rogue stories', and usually referred to in English translations as 'Dalilah the Crafty'. Seeing two thieves rewarded with salaried positions at court, the widowed Dalila decides to become a consummate thief. She robs several individuals—including the young wife of an Emir. Exposed, she gets vengeance by selling the complaining victims of her trickery into slavery. Arrested, she slips out of captivity and turns the tables on the two rogues who had been appointed captains of the caliphal guard—one of whom promises to have her acquitted if she returns her stolen goods. She does so, and secures a position and stipend.

That al-Bustani uses this epithetic reference is interesting, especially as it is put into the mouth of Boulos. Dalila's story is a tale of thievery and eluding the security authorities who are themselves former brigands. This figure is also linked to the 'wiles of women' theme found in such story collections and differently in the Qur'an. In al-Bustani's encyclopaedia, the entry for *Dalila* focuses entirely on the biblical Delilah: another possible source for the notion of a 'wily woman'.

24 *the property of . . . the family*: see note to p. 5.

25 *cryptic words*: Arabic *tilasm* (from the Greek *telesma*) from which the English word 'talisman' derives. As a charmed object than can release effects—with the power to protect or give—the talisman's force arises from the words written on or in it. This meaning in European languages emerged from the translation/adaptation of 'oriental tales' and particularly the *Thousand and One Nights,* especially the selections and rendering of the eighteenth-century compiler/translator Antoine Galland. But in Arabic, the term is used with a broader sense of mysterious words or meanings. *Tilasm*, in the Arabic text, may remind us that the presence of the mysterious in Arabic novels of the Introduction and this era was nourished not only by European Gothic but also, and more pervasively in most cases, by indigenous story-telling traditions. On *talisman*, see Marina Warner, *Stranger*

Magic: Charmed States and the Arabian Nights (Cambridge, MA: Belknap/Harvard University Press, 2011), ch. 10. As she comments, with relevance to our text, 'The writings on the talismans need not be legible; indeed they gain in efficacy through their enigma and resistance to decipherment' (p. 219). In a sense, the letters Lutfi receives are talismans: they seem to exert a magic power over him; they are not benign; and they do not bring good fortune.

27 *the tale of Geneviève with her husband:* Geneviève de Brabant (b. 680 CE?) was a figure of medieval Christian piety, sometimes said to have been sainted. The story went that she was falsely accused of adultery by schemers—one of whom wanted her as a sexual partner or wife—and was banished from home while her husband was away on a military campaign. She raised a child whilst living in the forest; and was finally exonerated but then, in some versions of the story, died of exhaustion. The book that Sa'iba is reading might be a Turkish translation of a popular German rendering by the prolific German author Christoph von Schmid (1768–1854), known especially for his books for young people. His *Genovefa* (1810) was translated into many languages. However, it is not clear that an Ottoman Turkish translation existed by 1891. Johann Strauss notes that the story of Geneviève de Brabant was sometimes confused with Lamartine's *Geneviève. Histoire d'une servante*, of which a translation into Ottoman was published in 1879. A Karamanlı (Ottoman Turkish in Greek script) translation existed as early as 1854, likely translated from a Greek translation (1846). (I am grateful to Johann Strauss for this information.) Perhaps, as a well-educated Ottoman, Sa'iba read the tale in French.

Al-Bustani could have read Schmid's rendering of the tale in her native tongue: his book was translated into Arabic and published in 1866 (Kristuf Shmid al-Nimsawi, *Kitab riwayat Jinfiyaf*, 'translated from the French to the Arabic by *al-khawaja* Mikha'il Jahashan, a student at the Greek Orthodox School in Beirut' (the title page lacks information on the publisher and date)). But, as a well-educated product of missionary schools, she could have read a translation, or another treatment of the tale, in English. For more on Geneviève's story as an intertext in this novel and how it intersects with al-Bustani's use of Gothic motifs—and on another possible source—see Appendix 2.

28 *Sunna of the Prophet... Right Path*: the 'Way' of the Prophet, his reported words and deeds, as an impeccable guide for behaviour and a source, along with the Qur'an, of knowledge on the faith and its social ramifications. Here, the reference is to the strictures on gender mixing and body covering as mentioned in the Qur'an (for both genders), and as explicated by narratives of the occasions when the pertinent verses were revealed to Muhammad. To this day, there is much discussion of whether these narrated occasions applied only to the wives of the Prophet or were meant as directives for all Muslims for all time, as there is a range of interpretations of what 'covering' and gender segregation actually mean in practice.

29 *sensible temperament*: the word translated here is *i'tidal*, 'moderateness', and the coupling of 'beauty' and 'moderateness' again points to the developing feminine ideal of the era as reformists saw it, underlined by the reference to an 'angelic' presence and the trope of 'light' suggesting an 'enlightened' character.

30 *nine o'clock European time*: the Ottoman day began at sunset; but the European time-labelling system was also used. Perhaps it is particularly mentioned here due to the presence of Boulos the Greek. But also, it delineates the image of Farid as a would-be Europeanized young Ottoman male. It is worth noting that 'respectable' evening entertainment was supposed to end about two hours after sunset. Farid's late hours mark him out as a wayward subject.

31 *ifranji time*: referring again to 'European time'. *Ifranji/afranji* was a term used in Turkish and Arabic, derived from 'Frank' or 'Frankish', signifying 'European' and used to refer to both people and 'Western' practices, objects, foods, etc. *al-Tarikh al-afranji* denotes the Gregorian dating system. In Turkish, the expression *alafranga* (< Italian *alla franca*) was used.

36 *military administration*: Ar. *al-sirr 'askariyya*; Tk. *serasker*, 'head of the army/soldiers'. Western sources refer to the War Ministry as Séraskiérat (Tk. *seraskerlik*).

the city of Salonica... a provincial police force: the populations of late nineteenth-century Salonica and its hinterland faced continuing insecurity of person and property for many reasons. Brigandage in the countryside had long posed a problem for the Ottoman authorities as well as for locals. With rising and competing nationalisms amongst Greek, Bulgarian, and Vlach populations, traditional brigandage—kidnapping for ransom, attacks on commercial caravans, and the like—increasingly became intertwined with political resistance and even organized insurgency (more intensively in the years after *Sa'iba* was published). As the Empire lost segments of its European territories, population migrations into the city intensified urban crowding, poverty, and resulting tensions that might lead to conflict and crime.

With conflict in and near the Balkans, Salonica became a military hub. In earlier times, it had been a military recruitment point for Muslim subjects from the surrounding area (Mazower, *Salonica*, 101). Large numbers of Ottoman army troops stationed in Salonica did not always improve the security situation for the city's (and hinterland's) inhabitants and indeed might contribute to instability. Aspects of urban development in Salonica were sometimes spurred by security concerns: for instance, gas street lighting was meant to deter crime (Anastassiadou, *Salonique*, 164). Mazower mentions a 'lack of police' in Salonica as hampering 'the monitoring of known trouble spots—cafés, cabarets, casinos' and quotes an unnamed individual as noting these as 'where all the wicked subjects gather to drink, play cards and gamble, and then prowl the streets' (Mazower, *Salonica*, 147). The local press carried many notices of petty crime and murder (ibid. 246).

In the city, the Muslim elite was preponderantly government-employed, including military officers and police; the military had a visible presence indeed in the city (Basil C. Gounaris, 'Salonica', *Review* (Fernand Braudel Center), special issue, 'Port-Cities of the Eastern Mediterranean 1800–1914', 16, no. 4 (Fall 1993), 499–518; Anastassiadou, *Salonique*, 4; Mazower, *Salonica*). Traditionally, policing had been organized locally. That Lutfi is sent from Istanbul alludes to the growing centralization of security functions in the Empire. The text uses the term *al-darrak* (*darak*, area of watch or patrol) from a root meaning 'to follow', and, in parentheses, the European term *al-bulis* (police). From earlier in the century, the governors Istanbul sent to oversee municipal matters and security were generally 'military men, trained to make war and to clean the region of brigands' (Anastassiadou, *Salonique*, 84; Booth's translation from the French). The city did not have a 'regular municipal police force till late in the century, and the streets were patrolled irregularly' (Mazower, *Salonica*, 146). Lutfi's mission, it seems, was to take over a new but inexperienced contingent of security personnel. However, although the text here has Lutfi instructed to go specifically to 'the city of Salonica' to assume security duties, it is actually a smaller provincial town to which he will go.

40 *both . . missed the mark*: this passage carries an interesting ambiguity. The author may be playing here with the name of her central character; *musib*, from the same linguistic root as *Sa'iba*, can mean 'pertinent' or 'correct' or 'on the mark', but it can also mean 'afflicted', often by something terrible (a *musiba*). The phrase in Arabic here is *musiban mukhti'an*; the rhetorical conjunction of opposites seems to offer a dominant sense: 'they were both on target, and they were both at fault/mistaken'—but with a harmonics of affliction, error as tragedy.

44 *took a boat to Salonica*: the railway that connected Salonica to Istanbul was completed in 1896; the rail link to Belgrade had opened in 1893. Thus, these crucial communications links were not yet in place when the novel was published.

a town situated in the interior of the province: in Chapter 7, Lutfi was ordered specifically to 'the city of Salonica' to manage the police. But taking on security in the hinterland—based, as he apparently is meant to be, in one of the smaller towns of the vilayet—was also a major concern for the Empire, and the setting provides a believable setting for the conflict that ensues.

The Macedonian hinterland was a rich agricultural area, yielding produce and other goods—particularly wool and silk—that were transported in caravans to Salonica for export within the Empire and, thanks to its lively port, internationally as well. Thus, the hinterland was important in both economic and political terms. When the railroads were built, Salonica's role as an entrepôt became even more important.

several parasangs: a *parasang* equals one *farsakh* (Pers., used in Ottoman and Arabic), or 6–8 km.

44 *well-shaded groves and fast-running streams*: the thickly forested interior to the north and east of Salonica did not have a developed road system at this time.

47 *wooden lattices*: known in Arabic as *mashrabiyya*, finely carved wooden window lattices were a ubiquitous feature of Ottoman and Egyptian urban domestic architecture—and often commented on by European visitors as well as featured in Orientalist paintings. They allowed light and air into the home, and permitted inhabitants to view the street, but they prevented passers-by from looking into the home's interior. They would cover windows overlooking the street in the family's private apartments (as opposed to the reception rooms designed for men of the family and their male visitors), and often also, windows facing onto an internal courtyard (if men might be present there). In this home, the reader learns that the windows facing the garden are not covered by lattices, since Soraya can see Sa'iba at her window as Soraya stands in the garden.

50 *As Molière said*: in a footnote in the novel, the author ascribes the Arabic translation of these lines to 'the honourable Sulayman Efendi al-Bustani'. Sulayman al-Bustani (1856–1925) was Alis's cousin (and, from 1897, her brother-in-law), the highly regarded translator of *The Iliad,* published in 1904 and received with immediate acclaim for its quality and its long, wide-ranging preface. He authored other works and would become member from Beirut of the Ottoman Chamber of Deputies (1908) and later a government minister.

I have been unable to trace either the original quotation or the translation; nor have colleagues who know Molière's work recognized this passage. Sulayman al-Bustani did not publish any translation of a Molière play; biographies mention generally that he translated texts from French while in school (personal communication from Yaseen Noorani, 19 January 2024). Perhaps his cousins had access to unpublished translations of his. Or, perhaps these lines (whether originally Molière's or not!) appeared in one of al-Bustani's many newspaper essays. Molière scholar Suzanne Jones suggests also that this might be from a song by Louis de Mollier, composer of *galant* song lyrics and poetry, his work sometimes wrongly attributed to Molière in nineteenth-century writings. The theme might be similar but no match for this passage has emerged (personal communication from S. Jones, 19 January 2024). I wonder whether it distantly echoes a line in *Le Misanthrope*, Act 4 sc. 1: 'Il aime quelquefois sans qu'il le sache bien, | Et croit aimer aussi, parfois quand il n'en est rien.' But if so, the translator has elaborated the meaning and changed the perspective from third to first person. The lines may also echo themes and diction of premodern Arabic poetry—for example, a line by Ya'qub al-Hajj Ja'far al-Tabrizi (1270–1329), a poet based in Najaf, Iraq: *ilayka wa-ma sha'ni al-gharam wa-madhhabi...*

The insertion of a *bon mot* said to be by Molière may suggest the milk-sisters' education was a somewhat cosmopolitan one. Although Alis was likely educated in English, French was an Ottoman language and would have been the European language most likely for these elite Ottoman Muslim females to study. Note that the character mentions the author's name here, unlike in the passages of premodern Arabic verse voiced by the narrating aunt.

52 *right conduct*: the Arabic phrasing here is a bit unusual: *idha ra'a ghayra shay'in zannahu rajulan*: 'if he were to see other than something he considers a man[s]'. In a novel that highlights middle-class urban young women as the pillars of social regeneration through sensible conduct and educated child-raising, the author uses the Arabic word *rajul* (man). A traditional metaphorical usage of this term signified 'perfect'—the bearer of the finest qualities; the one who can stand on his own without need of help; and connoting 'opposite of woman'. The impeccably sourced transmission of hadith—the Prophet's sayings and doings—was known as *'ilm al-rijal*, 'the science of men', even when the transmitter was female. Butrus al-Bustani's dictionary notes the metaphorical sense (*Muhit al-muhit*, 326).

53 *the bridge... toll for crossing*: this must refer to Galata Bridge, the main crossing between Fatih, in old Istanbul, and Beyoğlu, across the Golden Horn.

55 *their hiding places*: the paragraph alludes to the pervasive presence of brigandage, and crime generally, in the Macedonian hinterland. As noted earlier, this was a perennial challenge to the Ottoman government: when Sultan Abdülmecid made a state visit to Salonica in 1859, he was faced with petitions from subjects—urban and rural—asking help in suppressing brigand bands (Mazower, *Salonica*, 140). Crime was also proliferating from this time, entangled with political unrest, often expressed in terms of gang-based conflict and kidnappings. Anastassiadou remarks:

> In Ottoman Macedonia in the final decades of the nineteenth century—and especially in the interior—violence reigned endemically. The disaggregation of the imperial edifice was being lived daily. Along with 'political brigandage' practiced by clandestine independence groups, and spontaneous armed groups escaping all control, there was also ordinary criminality, civil disobedience, and an ongoing [atmosphere of] suspicion. (*Salonique*, 382; Booth's translation from the French)

And:

> Sometimes it was a matter of spontaneous banditry plain and simple, vaguely draped in nationalist ideas; other times, the Ottoman authorities had to contend with true guerrilla operations, carefully orchestrated.... In many cases, this was agitation by tiny groups whose influence barely surpassed the neighbourhood in which they were based. (Anastassiadou, *Salonique*, 389; Booth's translation from the French)

On political brigandage see also Mazower, *Salonica*, 260–3).

Weapons were rampant. Sources mention corruption in the context of brigandage: local police forces and other state personnel as well as local landowners often colluded with brigand groups. For a western European resident's view of brigandage and brigand society in the European provinces at the turn of the twentieth century, see Garnett, *Turkish Life.* 'Brigandage has from time immemorial, and more especially perhaps during the last century and a half, played an important part in the social and political life of Turkey, and the present anarchic condition of Macedonia offers every facility for the pursuit of this adventurous calling' (p. 208). Garnett describes vividly the facility with which gangs moved from one hiding place to another, often with the collusion of local residents.

60 *the hot baths at Bursa*: a reference to the famous hot baths in the old city of Bursa, on the south side of the Sea of Marmara, thus much closer to Istanbul than Salonica would be, and in an entirely different direction. (Given the Arabic spelling, alternatively this could refer to the village of Perissa on the island of Santorini, now in Greece, but this seems highly unlikely.) Bursa would be known to Arabophone readers as a venerable site of many historic mosques.

65 *as the poet has said*: this line of poetry closely echoes a somewhat more elegant line by the famous Shi'i Baghdadi poet al-Sharif al-Radiyy (970–1016 CE), from a prominent family descended from the Imam 'Ali, who was celebrated not only for his prolific and superb poetic corpus but for his honesty, loyalty, and freedom of thought—and intense pride in his own poetic output. Significantly, his love poetry is restrained and respectful, appropriate to the tone of this novel.

Al-Sharif al-Radiyy's line reads: حواجبنا تقضي الحوائج بيننا ونحن سكوت والهوى يتكلم

Our brows settle the needs between us
We are silence and it is passion that speaks

The novel's version is: لوائظنا تقضي المصالح بيننا فنحن سكوت والهوى يتكلم

MORE ABOUT **OXFORD WORLD'S CLASSICS**

American Literature

British and Irish Literature

Children's Literature

Classics and Ancient Literature

Colonial Literature

Eastern Literature

European Literature

Gothic Literature

History

Medieval Literature

Oxford English Drama

Philosophy

Poetry

Politics

Religion

The Oxford Shakespeare

TROLLOPE IN **OXFORD WORLD'S CLASSICS**

ANTHONY TROLLOPE

The American Senator
An Autobiography
Barchester Towers
Can You Forgive Her?
Cousin Henry
Doctor Thorne
The Duke's Children
The Eustace Diamonds
Framley Parsonage
He Knew He Was Right
Lady Anna
The Last Chronicle of Barset
Orley Farm
Phineas Finn
Phineas Redux
The Prime Minister
Rachel Ray
The Small House at Allington
The Warden
The Way We Live Now

A SELECTION OF **OXFORD WORLD'S CLASSICS**